Chalk *and* Cheese

Flyfishing on my French chalkstream

CHARLES HAMER

MERLIN UNWIN BOOKS

First published in the UK by Merlin Unwin Books 2020

Merlin Unwin Books Ltd
Palmers House
7 Corve Street
Ludlow
Shropshire SY8 1DB UK

www.merlinunwin.co.uk

ISBN 978-1-913159-22-1

Typeset in Minion Pro by Merlin Unwin Books
Printed in Great Britain by TJ International, Padstow, England

Contents

Prelude	5
Map	7
How it all Began	8
An Introduction is Made	9
I Learn to Fish	18
Level Two	28
Interlude	33
Paradise Lost	36
Paradise Regained	39
We Survey our Estate	43
L'Andelle	46
Sylvestre	49
Further Investigation	56
Estate Matters	59
Our Village	64
The Market Town	72
Bread	81
Normandy Snippets	84
River Walk	89
What had we Bought?	94
Early Sorties	98
A Mystery Solved	103
Further River Ramblings	107
More Fishy Things	115
French Rules and Red Tape	118
The Road Beat	121

Contents

The Ditch   125

Riparian Owners' Association   128

Building Works   132

Gardening   139

River Maintenance   143

Nature Watch   147

Putting the River to Bed   153

Postscript   159

Dedicated to my three girls.
Marthe who has put up with me for 42 years.
Sophie and Celia for encouraging me to write
this book, for being my fiercest critics and for
making sure I finished it.

Prelude

I am determined to avoid the most common clichés found in books (mainly) about fishing.

First I am not going to apologise for adding to the, already vast, numbers of fishing books.

There will be no tales of battles with great fish – won or lost.

At the risk of multiple repetition of the word 'fishing', I am not going to use 'angling' (simply because I dislike the word – pure prejudice). Equally, and for the same reason, there will only be fishermen, not fisherwomen.

Further, I am not going to quote poetry – partly because I don't know any and partly because, again, I don't like it.

There will be virtually no Latin, mainly because I have forgotten all I ever knew, despite many years of effort by my teachers at school, and anyway it tends to look a bit show-offish.

I know my limitations and have no pretensions to instruct the reader as to how to fish so there will be no instruction. Equally I will not discuss equipment, much as I love it – I am 'kit mad'.

It is hard to avoid the use of clichés when describing trout (speckled beauties etc) and water, but I've done my best to avoid them – mainly by not describing them at all. At least there are no chubs here to be called aldermen.

And there is no sex (except perhaps among trout).

If you can forgive all the above I hope you will enjoy this book. It has only come into being because my daughters have refused to let me stop. Forced by my health into an early retirement, I mentioned that I had better write a book to keep me sane, and my daughters have never forgotten that idle comment, and have constantly 'egged me on'. So you can thank them for the result – or not.

Charles Hamer

How it all began

New Year's Day 1994 saw the family assemble for its annual gathering at my mother-in-law's house. A little part of this ritual was playing out as always; Oncle Jean, after a little small talk (he wasn't long on chat), produced his diary from his inside breast pocket, apparently as an afterthought though it happened like that every year, and I knew what was coming next – or so I thought.

An Introduction is Made

We were first introduced to the Andelle in 1984 – and fell in love at first sight.

Before my (French) wife Marthe and I first visited Normandy, neither of us had any idea that there even *was* such a thing as a chalkstream outside the UK. Now we know there are two, the Risle and the Andelle, and that they can easily be compared with the Test and the Itchen respectively. A look at a map covering the south of England and the west of Normandy shows clearly how the two pieces of land would have been joined many millennia earlier and hence how the seam of chalk runs through both.

These two French rivers share all the traits of the true chalkstream: pure, clear, constantly cold water holding at a steady level, fed by the aquifers below. There is abundant weed growth and the classic fly life of these rivers, including, here at least, the mayfly.

The chief difference is in the number of beats still holding a head of wild fish without stocking. This is largely due to the lower pressure of fishing. Flyfishing is very much a minority sport in France and demand for such water is far less than in the south of England where fishing pressure is such that stocking is almost inevitable. The idea of returning fish to the river once caught arose as a concept too late to save the English chalkstreams from restocking.

In France it is rare for the pressure to be sufficient to necessitate introducing new stock. But access to that gem, an unstocked French chalkstream, is if anything even more difficult to attain than in England. The vast majority of these French beats are in private hands – private hands who would never think of letting day rods. The only way to fish these rivers is through one of the few clubs who lease beats and through whom it is sometimes possible to take a day or weekly rod. These beats are inevitably hard fished, as one would expect.

The haven to which we were introduced that June day was a stretch of some seven hundred yards of delightful chalkstream with all the variety one could crave. Flowing through lush water meadows, cropped by the pretty Norman brown and white spotted dairy cattle, with rapid areas flowing over sparkling gravel and slow 'S' bends depositing a little silt on their inner edges. This beat belonged to Marthe's uncle and we were invited for the weekend.

As the only other members of the family who fished, we were the lucky recipient of what became an annual invitation to fish the first weekend in June. This date had been identified over the years as being the height of the mayfly on this stretch of the Andelle and our best chance of success. The hatches were spectacular, fulfilling all the clichés used to describe them in fishing literature and which it is beyond my capabilities to improve upon. We were lucky indeed!

Those were the days before the building of the Channel Tunnel so we crossed by the night ferry from Portsmouth to Le Havre. This seemed, in a way, to make this even more of an adventure despite the torture of sea-sickness to which I am prone even at the sight of the Serpentine in Hyde Park. The ferry docked in the early morning around 6am and we later learnt to make straight for the nearest café to drink a large café crème with a croissant in order to quell the cold ache in the pit of the stomach induced by a sleepless night in a grim cabin and an early start. On this first occasion, however, we set off straight for the river.

The route took us through Rouen where we arrived just as the rush hour started. This is not an experience for the faint-hearted on their first visit to the city, which has an extensive network of one way streets including a 'speed-way' along the 'quais'. On top of this (as in France in general) the destination you were following on the signposts would suddenly disappear completely only to reappear just as you were sure you had gone wrong and were trying to make a U turn. Equally, little or no advance warning is given of the exit that you wish to take, with inevitable results. This situation is never helped by the habit in France of positioning signs at traffic lights only beyond the lights so that they are hidden if you happen to be behind a lorry.

By some miracle we negotiated this maze and came out on the right road. From there we travelled some twenty kilometres through a virtually flat and totally uninteresting plain until suddenly the ground opened up before us and we descended straight into the most perfect little chalkstream valley. It really was a perfect 'V' such as one imagined and painted as a child. Were it not for the advertising placards painted large on the ends of the first houses in all the villages, we could have been in Hampshire.

But we had arrived; passing the château (extensively publicised from miles around – the owner was an MP who controlled such things) we soon entered the village which had a rather run-down appearance, mainly due to the scruffy Routier right at the entrance. This had a huge and very empty car park and little sign of life. Then we swung down towards the river until we found the house and the welcoming aunt and uncle who had prepared a huge, and most unsuitable, breakfast of saucisson sec and pâté en croute – after all, Tante Maleine did come from Lyon!

The inner man dealt with, we strung our rods. Why is it I always find that everyone else seems to take an age to do this and that I am rigged up and itching to go long before anyone else and have to sit there twiddling my thumbs? But eventually we were under way.

Oncle Jean, slightly lame from birth, was not able to fish for long stretches of time and as a result I had the beat almost to myself as Marthe kept Tante Maleine company. At lunch on Saturday Oncle Jean was clearly pre-occupied and after some period of internal debate he decided to tell me the reason – he could not understand why I had not caught more than the one under-sized fish that I had grassed that morning. As it happened the same thing had exercised my brain too. My knowledge of trout fishing was very limited and was largely self-taught from books, as my grandmother, who was my fishing mentor, had just assumed I knew what I was doing when she took me on the river and I had been too shy to ask.

That June morning Oncle Jean had caught several fish in the short time he was on the river and at lunch said he had been watching me casting 'beautifully'. Thus he could not understand the size of my basket (of which more later). A quick inspection of my kit revealed that I had a straight, un-tapered leader such as I had always used for salmon fishing with which I was much more familiar. I had not known that the high-born, wild *Salmo trutta fario* of the Andelle were far too canny to accept such a coarse offering, however fine the casting. A quick change to a tapered leader provided by Oncle Jean and advice to the effect that 'you cannot strike too quickly' did the trick and the afternoon provided non-stop action as the mayfly was 'up' and now I was in tune with the trouts' desires.

That weekend (fishing is permitted on a Sunday in France – a bit of a surprise in a Catholic country) we caught 45 trout between us, with a little help from Marthe when she was let off duty, and from Tante Maleine who retired to the furthest end of the beat from whence she returned shortly after with three or four fish. It did not take long to realise that she was spinning, a heinous crime on a chalkstream, and that the reason she went to the far end was not out of any embarrassment, but because down there was to be found a stretch where she was not perpetually snagged on the bottom.

One of the few 'rules' given out the first morning by Oncle Jean was that all fish were to be kept unless really sardine-sized. To this end we were each armed with a metal contraption, a cross between a creel and a keep net, with a spring-loaded lid and to which a stake was attached by a length of baler twine. This basket was immersed in the river and pegged to the bank with the stake. It was then ready for action. All fish caught were put in this and kept 'alive' in the river until we came in for lunch or supper when they were all despatched by the cook. It remained a mystery to us what the aunt and uncle, who had no children, did with such numbers of fish. Sadly the fish were so stressed by being kept in such conditions (the baskets were small and there were often many fish in them) that by the time we returned to the house they were almost black in colour, and no doubt the flavour suffered too. Given this slaughter, it was astonishing to see the enormous number of fish still rising in the evening, particularly as these were all wild fish, the beat not having been stocked in living memory.

The house itself was a strange mixture of classic Norman colombage, (timber frame over a flint foundation and in-filled with cream render over an infill of horsehair, mud and so on) and rather strict and simple brick, all under a slate roof, The house had clearly evolved over the years with the different eras evident to the eye (and later confirmed by photographs) with one end having been the cattle byre. This was now the sitting room which led off a dining room which in turn acted as entrance hall. Over these two rooms were two double bedrooms, a tiny single room (which had been for the chauffeur in time gone by) and a shower room. Oncle Jean did not believe in the luxuries of life and the furnishings were simplicity itself with just some rattan chairs around the large and very ugly fireplace. This had been installed when the original works had been done in the 1950s and looked like it. The simplest dining table and chairs and ancient brass beds, which did however have glorious hollows into which one rolled to sleep the sleep of the dead, completed the furnishings.

No-one had spent much time or thought on decoration either, with the same wall-paper used in both bedrooms, albeit in a different colour. The curtains were made of a design of bull-rushes which Marthe immediately recognised, as her mother had bought a job lot on a Parisian market many years previously and this fabric had been used everywhere, by all members of the family, for everything from awnings for a wedding (ours) to, as we now knew, curtains in a fishing lodge. In fairness Oncle Jean and Tante Maleine did not come down very often and nor had the grandfather who had bought the property in the first place. The two cousins who ran the family firm at the time of purchase, one Marthe's grandfather, had had the reputation of leading a life for which many would give their right arm. Their working day reputedly consisted of going to the office in the morning, dictating a few letters and then spending the middle of the day either shooting or fishing before returning to the office at the end of the day to sign the letters and cheques. They had however done extremely well in business and, as was the way at the time, had invested their money in land, forestry and rivers – more specifically the Andelle – where they had bought three properties. These properties had been bought through the company and so eventually had to be separated out as the number of share-holders in the family business grew. And by this means Oncle Jean, as one of the beneficiaries, came to own this stretch. It was he who had made the house habitable with even an inside loo, installed at the time of the improvements in the early 1950s, whereas his grandfather had had to trek down to the bottom of the garden. We subsequently found a photograph of the house pre-improvements, showing the disposition of the various elements, not to mention a splendid, as yet unidentified motor car with rather flashy white-walled tyres.

The property was looked after by a husband and wife couple, Monsieur and Madame Cartier, who lived in one end (I really cannot call it 'wing') of the house. Monsieur supposedly was the riverkeeper but was so overweight and lazy that we were pretty certain that he never even reached the far end of the beat. Madame cooked the simple fare preferred by our hosts. There was a certain eccentricity in the arrangements in that there was no connecting door between the two ends of the house so that our meals left the kitchen, were carried outside, along the front of the house come rain come shine and then in through the dining room door. Inevitably they were not exactly piping hot upon arrival.

The Cartiers lived in their end of the house the whole year round and kept a few scrawny chickens who scratched around in a dusty run alongside their vegetable patch. As Jean only came down to fish the mayfly for three or four weekends a year, life was sweet for the Cartiers.

The weather that weekend was delightful. Warm and sunny (with just enough cloud for fishing convenience) and with only a light zephyr – so untypical of mayfly season as we generally know it where the wind always seems to howl downstream. The house stood just back from the river, a gentle meander of some one hundred yards beside the public water sufficing to bring you to the bridge over the river which marked the upstream end of the beat.

Oncle Jean had donated this stretch of water, which was nearest the village, to the commune where it became part of the public fishing for the locals. This presumably had been intended to reduce the temptation to fish his private water. Whether this had worked we were never really sure.

When too exhausted to go on catching fish – it really got to that – I lay in the water meadows and watched the cows being driven home to be milked or delighted in the antics of the water rats as they built their nests. It is amazing how far they will swim with a piece of reed in their mouths when there is one, apparently identical, far closer to home. It was truly idyllic – we had discovered paradise on earth.

17

I Learn to Fish

My own beginnings in fishing were very close to the clichéd 'bent pin and a jam jar' school of learning. However I was very lucky to have a grandmother who fished and therefore had real kit! There was something compulsive about the wonderful black japanned fly-boxes containing glorious, multi-coloured salmon flies the size of a sparrow, tied on gut eyes and which had probably been made for salmon fishing in Norway – I have pictures of various ancient relatives with enormous salmon, some of which I know were actually caught there. There were heavy brass reels that made a wonderfully satisfying noise when the line was pulled off, nets which still carried a slight whiff of fish alongside the mustiness of the cupboard under the stairs where these wonders were stored, and heavily varnished rods in their duck-cloth cases. I never tired of rummaging through this treasure trove, which included everything from croquet mallets to long-bows, and there an obsession was born that was to last to this day.

As a result when I first went to try for a fish, I actually had a rod, line and proper hook. The target species was not defined and the bait was a worm. This was suspended randomly into what was little more than a ditch that ran through the far end of my grandfather's farm. Nonetheless I caught a small 'something' which I carried home in triumph – in a jam jar (why do small boys carry jam jars if not for this?). Once paraded for the whole family to admire, this poor unfortunate creature was placed with great ceremony in the lily pond outside the drawing room window. Here it was found floating, belly-up, a few days later. But my love for fishing had begun.

Then came the less fun part of fishing. Those were the days of silk flylines and I was not allowed to do anything else until I had stripped the whole line off the reel to dry; to which purpose it was festooned around the hall, over the large, sagging sofa that served as a bed for the 'house' dogs, around chairs and chests of drawers and so on. The importance of this was drummed into me as the first thing to do on coming in from fishing, just as was cleaning a gun after shooting.

On the rather fine chest of drawers in the hall was an item which was also of endless fascination to a small boy. Alongside a no doubt once-priceless but now heavily-riveted Chinese bowl containing dog leads and whistles, stood a miniature, oak postbox. Complete with a label set in a silver mount giving the hours for collection of letters, this had been a present to my great grandparents from their faithful staff in celebration of their silver wedding anniversary, as was engraved on the silver band around the base. Presumably it had been to one of these servants that the duty of emptying the postbox fell – twice a day.

This fascination to the young endured through the years as I was later told that my aunt had caused pandemonium in the household by hiding the ration books in the postbox during the war. By then there was no longer a butler and the box was never opened. It was some time before she confessed.

Not long afterwards my grandmother presented me one Christmas morning with a long and exciting-looking parcel. I ripped off the wrapping with great haste to reveal – my very own rod! Clearly Granny had seen a budding, serious fisherman in me as this was a perfect split-cane rod, and to my scale. This delightful little 6'6" rod is still in my possession and is in perfect order to this day. It was made by A.E.Rudge of Redditch who, from what my research has revealed, made mainly coarse fishing rods, though this is a fly rod with a classic cane action. It still has the retailer's label from C.Jeffrey and Sons of Dorchester who were the local general sports shop and fishing outfitters at that time. Now I was a proper fisherman.

My grandparents owned a small farm in Dorset which was heaven for a young boy, providing endless interest in its hundred and fifty or so acres. As my father was still a serving soldier and seemed at the time to be perpetually stationed in Germany, I spent a lot of school holidays on the farm.

To the left on entering the property and some two hundred yards from the main house was an old cobbled stable yard of some half dozen loose boxes (horses long gone) and a tack-room which still had the unique smell of damp leather and faint traces of saddle soap – though sadly the remaining tack could have used the application of some. The particular shade of a rather bright green used for all the exterior paint-work on the stables and throughout the farm has remained clear in my memory to this day. These buildings held a great attraction for me which I still cannot explain, given that they were only used on rare occasions and mainly as whelping boxes for the Labradors and I have never liked riding.

My grandmother kept chickens, by now for laying, but once they had been for showing – a frame of splendid medals won by her flock was propped up in the dining room. My brother and I were given the task of searching the coops for eggs and the mystery porcelain eggs in the roosting boxes which were never explained to us except to the extent that they were not edible. These chickens were truly 'free-range' as they had an enormous run in which to forage until shut up at night, safe from marauding foxes. We were also tasked with broadcasting the feed in great handfuls taken direct from the wooden-handled tin measure.

Set into the outside of the lower ground floor of the house was a very dark feed room which contained the large galvanised bins for the chicken meal, for dog meal and biscuits. My brother and I were terrified of this gloomy place because of a very large, ferocious-looking but moth-eaten, stuffed boar's head which hung above the feed bins, tusks gleaming and apparently ready to charge – the result of Grandpa's pig-sticking exploits when on service in India. Grandpa was a soldier, in common with, it seemed, every male member of my family on both sides and including those who had 'married in'.

For the dogs, there was always an evil smelling cauldron perpetually bubbling away on the range. Into this witches' brew went everything and anything – but the dogs didn't seem to care, and at least it softened the biscuit for the older dogs lacking the full set of teeth.

The house had its own water supply from a natural spring which was pumped up. It stood high in its grounds and from it one could just see the sea on a good day. The pump house was a source of wonderment. Strictly off limits to us children, it was naturally irresistible. Our only way to see the great, smelly, and very noisy pumping engine was to peer through the grimy window on tiptoes, through which little could be seen, or to wait for the gardener to open up to service or repair the monster – not an infrequent occurrence. Just below the pump house was the well itself which was just an open, round pool of deep water over which was a very flimsy iron grating which would almost certainly not have been sufficient to save any of us foolish enough to walk on it. However the stories of the immense depth of this water did the trick and none of us ever fell in.

Next door to the pump house was the potting shed which, like the tack room, I can still smell in my memory

– an evocative combination of compost, creosote, broken crocks, tarred string and paint. There always seemed to be badly closed tins of paint, drips down the sides (usually of the aforementioned estate green) stacked on a high shelf alongside jam-jars full of labels, and assorted tempting containers with the irresistible skull and cross-bones, and the word 'Poison'. Mole traps hung from a nail above flower-pots full of bamboo canes for staking the herbaceous borders and next to these stood an ancient machine, covered in splashes of whitewash, which was used for marking the lines on the grass tennis court, which was set on the main lawn, well below the house. A series of stone terraces led down to this through extensive planting on randomly paved steps with plants self-seeding gleefully in the gaps between the stones.

Beyond the tennis lawn, which doubled-up for croquet, was a pond, complete with island, which was my grandfather's pride and joy and which he had had dug. Quite why I was never sure, but the likeliest explanation was that he intended to eventually shoot duck off it though I never saw this plan come to fruition.

My grandfather raised a few pheasant poults to put down for the family shoot, a walk round for three or four of us with a couple of his wild spaniels – 'Come here you bloody dog' was the familiar cry. But in his eyes 'his' dogs were always superior to my grandmother's immaculately behaved Field Trial Champion Labradors.

Secretly his real love was an extremely naughty Pekinese named Puff which terrorised my brothers and me, standing at the top of the stairs ready to bite our ankles for no other reason than that she could. Further, our attempts to outflank her by using the back stairs never worked either – she got there first! But Puff did tricks under orders from my grandfather for which she was rewarded at every turn with chocolate drops. It was totally out of character for this strong, silent, outdoors man to dote on a lap-dog.

He drove round the local lanes in a battered old Austin van painted a shade of green not unlike that of the stable doors. A ride with him was a terrifying experience as his unique approach to dealing with a cross-roads was to blow his horn a long blast as he approached and to cross without looking left or right, regardless of right of way, which he considered was always his. Miraculously he never had an accident.

Grandpa swore that his method of weather forecasting was infallible and far more reliable than the wireless. He hung a piece of seaweed from a nail in the porch and from the humidity of this he confidently predicted what was to come. History does not relate whether he was right and I was too young to remember.

It was in this child's paradise that I first shot a gun as well as caught my first fish. There was an ancient, hammer .410 which subsequent experience with my grandmother's 28 bore suggests was probably extremely dangerous, but I was allowed to use it to shoot rabbits once my grandfather had drummed the safety rules into me. Like every boy, I just wanted to get on and shoot but he made me carry the gun, unloaded, and to open it when climbing a fence or opening a gate for quite a long time before this was allowed. Those lessons were never forgotten.

My grandfather was the youngest of a family of nine brought up in a rambling old house, also in Dorset, where sport ruled. His father kept a large stable ranging from hunters through point-to-pointers and carriage horses to ponies, so the children learnt to ride from an early age. The same applied to fishing and, above all, shooting – a gun was kept propped up on the window seat of the school room (the children were tutored at home) and the boys and, just as much, girls were allowed to interrupt lessons if a rabbit was foolish enough to appear on the lawn during Latin translation. I was the beneficiary of this upbringing as he gave me the same opportunities.

One of his brothers, Eustace, carried this dedication to sport to extreme lengths as described in his book *Round the Smoking Room Fire* in which he fishes and shoots his way round the globe, chiefly at others' expense. This entertaining read is long out of print but is seemingly sought-after given the price it, and his other titles, fetch when they do appear on the market. To my amazement some years ago, my friend Chris Wates told me this tome had been his favourite read as a boy – I had never for a moment imagined that the book was known outside the immediate family.

Years later I was instructed by my grandmother when staying with her to shoot any rabbits I saw from the bedroom window. A weapon was provided in the form of the aforementioned 28 bore, appropriately also propped up on the window seat. A rabbit spotted on the lawn below, I duly loosed off. Whereupon flame shot sideways out of the breach nearly taking my eyebrows with it and certainly giving me an almighty shock. The rabbit was totally unmoved. The gun I condemned forthwith as lethal.

Once trained to Grandpa's satisfaction I did occasionally get invited to local shoots. Most were on a small scale, but great fun, These afforded me an introduction to many local landowners and thus to further opportunities (some unimaginably grand to a small boy) to shoot and fish. Fishing progressed rapidly from my first childhood experiences to fishing a 'proper' river. The Frome in those days still had a reasonable run of salmon, many of considerable size (25-pounders were not uncommon) and my grandmother had a rod one day each week. I often tagged along with a trout rod but still really had little idea what to do.

The salmon fishing was difficult, to say the least, as there was extremely luxuriant weed growth leaving the smallest channel in which to chuck the assorted ironmongery then in use. There was no question of using a fly – and if a fish was hooked the fun had only just begun. Nonetheless my grandmother occasionally seemed to manage to land a fish and indeed in her records, which I still have, she caught at least one fish a year right up until she was well into her eighties, despite very few opportunities. I was to be allowed the occasional 'chuck' with the very short fibre-glass spinning rod that she preferred. She insisted on using this 'toothpick' even when fishing the smartest beats in

Scotland, much to the disdain of the ghillies – until, that was, she wiped everyone's eye! She was a superb fisherman and inspired me to follow in her footsteps and continue a family tradition – her aunt had also been a fine fisherman and had the remarkable record of having landed two salmon, each over 40lbs and a third of 18lbs on the same day and with the same fly.

As an aside my grandmother never carried a landing net when trout fishing but would send one of her superbly-trained yellow Labradors to retrieve the fish. Their soft mouths ensured that the fish were never damaged – this was in the days before catch and release and the usual way to land a salmon was with a gaff which horribly disfigured the catch, so the dogs performed the same duty, better. These dogs all descended from 'Ben of Hyde' bought by my great grandfather from a fishing boat in Poole Harbour – the first yellow Labrador ever imported to Great Britain.

Level Two

On rare occasions my father fished with my grandmother and it was he who helped take my 'career' to the next level. My parents started to take a week or two in Scotland every year, initially in the classic way of renting a lodge with a mixed sporting estate – grouse, a stag or two, 'chance of a salmon' (only in the agents literature) and a loch for brown trout. This is something we subsequently started to do with our own children who have, to a degree, inherited our passion for fishing.

The first of these lettings was a small (for Scotland) estate named Scardroy in Strathconnon. The lodge was a modest, single storey building of no distinction set up above a loch at the very end of the glen accessed by a lengthy single track road. The glen is the longest in Scotland at some twenty miles and it was a tortuous drive of about forty minutes from the main road at Muir of Ord. I believe this old lodge has been replaced in recent times. By far the most interesting thing about the lodge was the wonderful run of game books belonging to the old General who then owned the estate. These recorded fishing catches and shooting bags going back many years on his various properties. One thing that sticks in my memory was a number of entries of shoots with bags in excess of a thousand hares on a single day.

There were a modest number of grouse reportedly on the moor and we had the right to shoot some 20 brace if memory serves. To this end my grandmother had borrowed two splendid old and steady pointers from Lord Rank, a friend who at the time was famed for his kennel of these dogs. I soon decided that it was far too much like hard work chasing these few birds round the hill.

I quickly realised that the Argocat never took us nearly far enough and that this sport always seemed to involve struggling through knee-high heather in steaming hot conditions and always uphill – and I was unfit. I confess that nonetheless this was very exciting shooting – I woke during the night on several occasions with my finger twitching on my imaginary trigger, so quickly did the coveys dip over the brow of the hill on which they always seemed to be strategically feeding. The tension when approaching cautiously behind one of the old dogs on the point was tremendous. The pointers were so steady we often had to physically push them forward to flush the birds.

Thus I deserted the moor and the rest of the party to spend many hours catching the tiny trout, known as 'breakfast fish' from the loch over-looked by the lodge. I even tried my hand (with a trout rod) at catching the 'chance of a salmon' – without success. Nonetheless it was clear to me and to my parents that it was the fishing that I loved.

The holidays progressed from the all-round estate to taking a house with a stretch of salmon river nearby (or usually the other way round and not so near). My father, who was as 'kit mad' as I later became, equipped my brother and I for our first attempt at 'proper' salmon fishing. I am certain he got as much pleasure out of buying as we did in receiving a 12-foot fibreglass rod with a reel, spare spool and floating and sinking lines (plus a tie-on sink tip). We thought we were 'the business'.

The extent of our instruction consisted of a short chat over a drink the night before starting out. The river that we first fished and to which we returned again and again, despite several abortive trials of other beats, was the Perthshire Garry. This river was apparently ruined by a hydro scheme in the 1950s but we had an autumn fortnight at which time there was almost always water.

Having reconnoitred the beat the day before (Sunday) my brother and I were far too excited to wait while our mother made our 'pieces' for lunch-time, so set off on our own to the river, some forty minutes' drive away. We crossed the railway line, in those days a simple matter of opening and shutting gates, now much complicated by Health and Safety, drove down to the hut, which was situated more or less in the centre of the beat, and got out of the car to set up our rods. As I stepped out of the driver's seat I saw a salmon fly on the ground (a Thunder and Lightning as I now know) and thought that this was fate. I strung up my rod and tied on this stray find, marched down to the pool in front of the hut and 'cast' about fifteen feet out. An extremely stupid or short-sighted salmon managed to shoulder through the coils of line and hook itself. It even made the playing pretty easy too, cruising slowly around for a bit before allowing itself to be towed unceremoniously up the convenient and gently inclined gravel beach on which I stood – I landed a 10lb salmon with my very first cast and was myself 'hooked' for life. Talk about beginner's luck!

I caught two more salmon that holiday whereas my brother, also on his first attempt, lost the two he hooked and has never gone salmon fishing again. I learnt an important lesson that year – it is very important for a beginner to have some success relatively early on. This is a lesson we applied to our own daughters when they took up fishing, inveigling a wonderful old Colonel, who was a knowledgeable fisherman as well as having a magical touch with children, to take them to a 'put and take' fishery and ensure they caught a fish. Both continue to fish to this day.

I fished this same beat every year for the next 35 years, taking on the beat when my father gave up the lease. It was an autumn fortnight and the fish were on the 'red' side but we knew no better to start with and could afford no better when we did know. The great thing was that we always saw a lot of fish, some of enormous size, something that I have always found hugely encouraging when salmon fishing – and one certainly needs all the encouragement going when trying for this elusive fish. Some years we even managed to catch quite a few fish and were only actually blanked once, which was pretty remarkable over such a period and given the tales of woe from many, much better-known (and more expensive) rivers.

After our marriage, Marthe joined us on these annual jaunts and immediately showed that she was an excellent fisherman – her first salmon was larger, at 17 ½ lbs, than any I have caught to this day. It was a fish certainly determined to break her duck for her, as she hooked him three times in quick succession, with the hook thrown twice before she drove the barb home – she was spinning at the time. It was a great stroke of luck that I had married someone who loved fishing as much as I did. She had to learnt to cast from Les Quais on the banks of the Seine in Paris, the thought of which always makes me smile.

But I digress; this is supposed to be a book about trout fishing.

Interlude

From this remarkable introduction to salmon fishing I found my interest in game fishing in general on the increase and I rapidly came to the conclusion that the Rolls Royce of fishing was the upstream dry fly, ideally on a chalkstream – a view I hold to this day. There is surely nothing to compare with the thrill of actually seeing a wild brown trout rise through several feet of crystal-clear water to take your fly (ideally one you tied yourself) having previously given it a thorough inspection and accepted its veracity.

I was still essentially self-taught, as my father was not a patient teacher and was an impatient fisherman to boot. I have always been lucky enough to have the knack of being able to teach myself from books (and careful observation of experts where available). This is fortunate as I take instruction badly! And so I set about improving my dry-fly technique. I also began to teach myself to tie flies – from a book of course.

Fortunately for me, my father had taken a rod one day a week at Timsbury on the Test and often took me as his guest. Furthermore whenever he was unable to fish it himself, he allowed me to go in his stead. This beat was heavily stocked so I cannot pretend that the fish were difficult, but at least I had the opportunity to practise and learn the basics. To show the extent of this stocking I caught one fish of 6 ½ lbs, such a slab that I seriously doubted that my net was big enough to take it, but it gave no fight at all and allowed itself to be towed straight over the waiting net into which it flopped with its tail hanging over the frame. When I laid it out in front of the hut at the end of the day the keeper looked at it and said 'that fish probably went in a week ago at 7 ½ lbs'. This was somewhat deflating.

After my father died I inherited the remainder of his lease, but when it ended I did not renew it – mainly for financial reasons. Kind friends invited us to fish various days on many of the best rivers in southern England and we reached the stage of being sufficiently competent not to embarrass ourselves and to grow increasingly passionate about this wonderful sport.

I started to read about all aspects of fishing and devoured the classics: Lord Grey, Plunkett Greene, Negley Farson, Ransome *et al* – and the passion grew. All this inspired the beginnings of a collection – I am an inveterate collector – and I believe that there have been more books written on the subject of fishing that any other sport, thus providing endless possibilities for a theme. Having started with the classics of the genre, the book that really sparked the beginnings of a library was a chance meeting with Thomas McGuane's *The Longest Silence* which I found in a hotel bedroom and which was for sale in the shop in Reception. Incidentally I have found that, to my taste at least, contemporary American authors on the whole write better about fishing than anyone else and I've always wondered why. I apologise profusely to the many excellent authors from elsewhere for this sweeping generalisation. Soon however I realised that I had to channel my collecting a little and grudgingly decided to concentrate on trout fishing. To date, and without too much searching, this library has extended to some two hundred and fifty books, showing just how many there must be in all.

It was then that fortune smiled on us and Oncle Jean first asked us to fish in Normandy. This heavenly invitation was extended regularly for nearly ten years thereafter.

Paradise Lost

I refer you, kind reader, to my opening paragraph of this story. The year was 1994 and 1st January saw the annual gathering of my wife's clan for lunch hosted by my mother-in-law. I held my breath waiting for Oncle Jean to approach me with his usual invitation for the beginning of June. This was usually prefaced by 'Have you got your diary with you, Charles?' Of course I had! But this year there was a surprise in store and it was not a pleasant one.

'Would you both like to come and fish for a few days? I am afraid, though, that it will be the last time'.

Oh my God! What had we done? I racked my brain but could think of no ghastly faux pas we had made.

Oncle Jean was a reticent man of few words, and no explanation was immediately forthcoming, so it was down to me to find out where it had all gone wrong. I was as much at a loss for words as he was and I think that all I said was:

'Oh? I am sure we would love to come'.

Clearly he could see my unspoken questions written all over my face and he, in his turn, was at a loss for words:

'I have sold the house'.

'Oh?' again.

We had both run out of our very few words.

After circulating for a bit, speaking mondanités to my in-laws, with my mind reverberating with the shock-waves of this bombshell, I approached Jean, determined to save the situation. Marthe and I had been in love with this place from the moment we set eyes on it and had dreamt of owning it one day – though quite how had never been clear – and I could not let it slip away without doing everything within my power to stop it.

'Oncle Jean, if you are ever thinking of selling, I would very much like to buy the house – you know how much we love it'.

I had absolutely no idea how we were going to pay for it if he had said 'Yes'.

It was his turn to be stunned.

'I am afraid I have already agreed to sell it to someone else'.

That was it then. He was a man of his word and he would never go back on such an agreement however much he might want to. Clearly he had never even considered that we might be interested, which was very surprising as we were the only members of the family who fished, who were invited there regularly at prime time and who had never refused an invitation. Marthe cut to the core of the matter when we discussed it later: 'As far as Oncle Jean is concerned, England might as well be as far away as Australia.'

I argued that he could not see it like that as, if it was so far away, how did we so readily accept the invitations year after year and furthermore travel over for just a weekend? In those early days, the journey was quite an undertaking but we were young then and kilometres did not frighten us. Nowadays it can take as little as five hours door to door to our home in London and, even better, in retirement we were able to make the trip mid-week, thus avoiding the worst of the traffic.

But it was no good, he never travelled himself, he didn't like 'nasty abroad', his brother looked after the export markets and we lived in 'Australia'!

Paradise was lost.

Paradise Regained

Subsequently we discovered that the sale was to be to another uncle who owned a beat about a kilometre below and who was buying it for his daughter and her fishing-mad husband. This compounded the certainty that we would never see it again. The logic of the purchase was unarguable from so many points of view. Through gritted teeth I congratulated Remy on his good fortune though I was unable to completely conceal my envy. Subsequent events suggested that this may have been a good thing.

I was so devastated at seeing our heaven disappear that I persuaded Marthe that we had to buy a property with fishing – and clearly with prices as they were at home it would have to be in France. Although everyone in France is a fisherman, it is mostly coarse fishing and the premium for flyfishing bears no resemblance to such as one finds in England. I dragged Marthe all over Normandy looking at totally unsuitable properties which claimed to have fishing but which varied from fifty yards of respectable fly-water to several hundred yards of heavily over-grown ditch three feet wide and which had never harboured a trout. I managed to persuade myself that a few days with a digger could soon transform this latter into a stretch of the Itchen and even came close to buying this property. With it came a gloomy, over-priced, half renovated mill which belonged to an English couple trying to escape from the mounting bills of the restoration. Luckily we did not proceed!

Two years later Remy rang us and said that they had decided to sell (no reason given) and would we be interested? He was backing a racing certainty as he knew we both fished and he had seen our faces that January 1st! Despite the much inflated price I was determined not to let this slip through our fingers again and would have paid more or less anything to acquire it. The much lower prices for French property and the exchange rate at the time did not make it seem too bad. Some to-ing and fro-ing later we had an agreement to buy and were sitting in the 'notaire's' office in Ry, the local market town.

Buying a property in France is very different from in the UK. My memory of the whole process is a little hazy with the passing of time – not least because I was on cloud nine – but we sat opposite each other for what seemed an eternity as the entire contract was read through, word for word. The 'notaire' in France can act for both sides, which has its advantages but, it seems to me, must lead to a potential conflict of interests. One clause which particularly amused me at the time, but proved later to be apposite, stated that the property benefitted from electricity and running water. This is covered indirectly in contracts in England but it seemed strange at the time to have it read out loud to us and in such precise terms.

Oncle Jean had originally sold what amounted to a small-holding with some fifty acres of grazing, but the contract we were to sign only concerned the house and, most importantly, the fishing. Jean had been shrewd and had protected the fishing by making of it a separate parcel with two metres of bank included so that the owner of the farmland did not have any fishing rights and that the buyer of the fishing had access to it – not a point to be ignored. When a large scale map was produced as confirmation of the detail of the deal my mind drifted back to reality and I concentrated. There was a bonus! We were buying two stretches of river that we had no idea were included and which we had never visited, let alone fished, despite our many stays there.

We had inadvertently acquired a second stretch of some one hundred and fifty yards of single bank fishing a little downstream and a length of what looked on the plan to be a length of carrier running arrow-straight next to the road and parallel to the main river (in as much as anything straight can be parallel to a typically serpentine chalksteam).

The papers signed and a glass of champagne drunk with our cousins back at the house, we were ready to retire for the night – it had been a long day, having left London that morning, and we were exhausted. Trying to wash before bed we found we had no water and no electricity so, too tired to try to resolve the problem then and there, we found a candle, crept upstairs, climbed into bed and fell into a deep sleep almost instantly.

I woke in the middle of the night with the hairs on the back of my neck standing on end – there was someone in the house or it was haunted – I could hear heavy footsteps apparently above our heads. A search by candle revealed nothing so I fell back into a listless sleep. There was a lot we had to learn about our purchase!

We Survey our Estate

We awoke to address the problems – always harder without a bath and a shave, I find. As it transpired, the solving of them both proved to be the work of moments. One look at the fuse box told me that the main fuse had tripped and with the flick of a switch we had power. We had momentarily forgotten that the house was not on mains water and that it came from a bore hole – via a pump which was, naturally, driven by electricity – so the one action had cured both our ills of the night before. We felt much better and would not need to call on the terms of our contract stating we had bought a house with water and electricity!

After our first breakfast at home – it felt great to call it that at last – we set out to see what we had bought. As we knew the house of old and were buying a property that had been in the family for generations, we had not bothered with any kind of survey and had not even visited it properly before writing the cheque. We were in for one or two surprises which were not as pleasant as the extra fishing we had acquired.

The part of the house that Oncle Jean had used we knew well and was largely unchanged. Downstairs was a hall and a sitting room out of which an open oak staircase led up to two double bedrooms, a tiny single room and a spartan shower room.

There had in the interim been some improvements made to the living area, not least the knocking through between the old keeper's quarters and the part of the house we had known. We had never actually set foot in the other half and had merely glimpsed from outside the interior of the main ground floor room which had served as living room, dining area and kitchen, with a huge old cast iron range. This had been converted to form a kitchen/dining room leading through a door in the pine panelling and up a couple of steps to a new bedroom and bathroom more or less at ground floor level, built into the old stable and above the cellar which was only half below ground level. Beyond this we had no idea what to expect.

Investigating further we climbed a steep, narrow, winding staircase and found ourselves in the nicest room in the house but one which clearly had not been used for a very long time. Panelled in pitch pine and with a double aspect, this room had a lovely view down to the river and we immediately knew this would be our bedroom. From the large number of huge nails driven into the beams we deduced that this had been used to hang the hams for curing – was this the source of the peculiar smell that we sensed in that part of the house? Later it took me a full day's work just to remove all these nails.

Now to investigate the rest of the building. A stable door led to what was now used as the wood shed and to our biggest shock yet. The back wall of the house was entirely held up by metal Acrow props! A door led through to a garage which seemed sound. The cellar was clearly pretty damp and contained the water pump and a large number of, sadly empty, champagne bottles. That completed the tour. We returned inside to face up to the fact that we had not just a gentle redecoration job but a serious re-building task on our hands.

The house runs more or less north-south meaning that only the evening sun shines directly into the main rooms. This ensures that the interior is wonderfully cool in the summer. It is also very cold in winter so it is fortunate that we are seldom there during the coldest months.

The building is one room deep for most of its length and, with very few exceptions, the windows all look west over the river valley with no other dwellings in view. One has no feeling of being on the edge of a village, an impression strengthened by the fact that there is no road noise as the house sits down below the road with plenty of trees and buildings to deaden the sound.

L'Andelle

Shaken to our roots by the fact that the whole of the east-side of the house was propped up on poles, we decided to cheer ourselves up by surveying the river – surely it couldn't be as bad? To our relief it wasn't, and fully lived up to our expectations. Our memories proved to be no mere dreams, it was a perfect chalkstream in glorious condition with the weeds abundant, but not too abundant. Sparkling gravel bars, a perfect mix of fast, shallow water and slow, deep pools of open water, deep shade and everything in between. Given Oncle Jean's insistence that all fish should be taken out and as a result the large numbers killed – there had been literally hundreds just on the few days we had been there over the years – the big question was whether there were any fish left? Only time would tell. Certainly during our survey that day we didn't see a single fish though we were of course well aware of the trout's uncanny knack of disappearing before one's very eyes.

All fishing in Oncle Jean's time had been from the right bank which proved to be a logical decision for several reasons. For most right-handers, fishing upstream is easier off the right bank and furthermore, whilst we owned both banks along the vast majority of the beat, there was a small length of the left bank that was not ours. In all the time we have owned this stretch we have only once seen the owner (and occasional poachers) fishing this short stretch of the other bank. To complete the reasoning there was also a stretch of heavily wooded bank which would not have been fishable from the other bank and there were very few trees on the right bank (probably the result of work over the years to improve the fishery). Access therefore meant crossing the river from the house via a bridge kindly provided, and maintained, by the commune – and thereby hangs another tale.

One stretch of 'free' water that we had acquired proved to be some two hundred and fifty yards of shallow, fast-flowing water heavily over-hung by stream-side reeds and tussocks of that notoriously fly-grabbing reed fishermen all know so well. Research later showed that this was no carrier but a separate river, L'Echelle. We thought little more of it at the time as it was extremely narrow and heavily 'poached' by the cattle having crossed and re-crossed along its length. Time was to show that we were wrong to ignore it.

Where the two rivers met, at the downstream end of our stretch, was a heavily over-grown and dilapidated hut which was almost invisible, hidden as it was in the trees and covered with brambles of spectacular size. This reminded us that there had been another, identical hut half way down the main river. We later discovered that it had been burned down by local boys 'amusing' themselves. Their amusement had also involved throwing the 'Pêche Gardée' signs into the river and an attempt to do likewise with the locked gate that gave access to the fishing. We later decided that such a gate was no bar to the local lads and indeed tended to encourage them to poach and so we never replaced it.

Here and there along the banks were some small benches which were barely wide enough for two slightly stout fishermen to sit side by side and they were painted white which gave them a very suburban look. As we returned homeward we encountered a short, nut brown, fit-looking man walking purposefully towards us. We were about to meet our inherited keeper, the man responsible for these benches and someone who was to have a great influence on our life at Cercy.

Sylvestre

Nut brown of skin, shock of white hair, dressed in a camouflage jacket and shorts and toting a .22 rifle, Sylvestre was a fairly intimidating figure, despite his short stature, and he seemed to lack only a bandolier of bullets slung across his chest – or maybe two, in cross-belts form – to become the perfect bandit. Later on, within moments of hearing his Christian name, our daughters christened him Stallone, and it was so appropriate, it stuck. To this day we have to remind ourselves not to use this nick-name to his face.

I do not think we ever actually formally engaged him with a contract but from that day forward he worked for us in the guise of riverkeeper and, for a time, gardener.

With the retirement of the Cartiers, Sylvestre had taken over the duties of keeper but had never lived in. He lived some twelve miles away and was nominally in charge of several beats on the Andelle thus apparently spending much of each day on the road up and down the river. This made his whereabouts unpredictable which was excellent for keeping the poachers on their toes, as much of the river could be seen from the road. Our predecessors had kept him on and there never seemed to be the slightest doubt in anyone's mind that we would do the same.

A riverkeeper in England would not be impressed by the work Sylvestre considered necessary to merit this title. His official duties consisted of keeping down the water vole population (thriving) and patrolling the river from time to time to keep off poachers. Later we decided that this latter duty was carried out a good deal more frequently when we were in residence. Everything else seemed to be 'extra'. These duties corresponded with his own preferred occupations, essentially of killing pests, or threatening to kill people. In fairness he was good at both!

He had been the maintenance man in a factory for many years before being made redundant and hence could turn his hand to almost anything and produce a superb result. In due course we were to get him to construct new benches on the river bank and they were so solid I am sure they will still be there long after we are gone. The problem was that everything he did was with such precision that it took many hours and therefore cost a fortune.

The same approach was taken to gardening and led eventually to our falling out, almost permanently. He would cut the hedges with such precision you would swear he had used a spirit level and a pair of nail scissors, leaving a manicured look that was totally inappropriate for our rural setting, at least to our eyes. This, we discovered in due course, is a very Norman trait, the locals all liking everything to be trimmed to the millimetre. When we asked him to be less precise he took umbrage and stormed off. Only the greatest diplomacy managed to prevent a full and final rift over this, though he gardened for us no more.

Trapping the water rats (voles) was something he loved. A series of galvanised steel 'run through' traps were situated at appropriate points along the beat and baited with carrots, which seemed to be the delicacy of choice as he never used anything else and continued to be successful, killing on average over a hundred water rats each winter. For a very long time we never received a bill for these carrots until one day we were charged with such a huge quantity that we assumed we had fed the whole village for years.

It seemed incredible to him when we told him that there were people in the UK actually re-introducing these cute creatures to first class rivers. He even suggested that we should start to sell our excess to these madmen. Once we had seen the damage caused by a combination of the burrows dug into the banks by these rodents, when combined with cattle treading them in from above, we could only agree with him. Once trapped, he despatched his prey with the .22 and tipped them into the river – natural habitat enrichment. He waged a constant battle with a local resident who lived close to the river and who, at the sound of a shot, would storm into her garden hurling abuse – I think he rather enjoyed it. The war against these pests was never won, despite his best efforts, as the stretches upstream and downstream were not keepered and so we were merely providing new territory for incomers.

He would also occasionally capture a coypu, a creature previously unknown to us. I shall never forget the first time I saw one in the river. Lying motionless and half-submerged in the middle of the river was an animal the size of a cocker spaniel. I sat and watched it for some time before disturbing it, sending it diving out of sight – but not before I had seen its rather ugly head with prominent, yellow incisors. Much waving of arms and attempts to describe this to Sylvestre elicited the probability that it was a *ragondin* which my grandmother's *Larousse* and an ancient French-English dictionary revealed to be a coypu.

Although both they and the water rats are herbivores and thus cause no difficulties to the trout population per se, those who have never encountered them cannot conceive of the harm they do to the river banks. Kenneth Graham has much to answer for by making one of these creatures so adorable, despite giving the vole the less than attractive name of 'Ratty'. On the back of this subject we learnt Jean Claude's grasp (or lack of) of the internet and indeed spelling. We received an email back in London, clearly sent from his wife's account, and typed without capitals, punctuation or sentences. This email was to warn us of the spread of the 'rats godin' following a wet winter. It took a moment to grasp what he was talking about but we enjoyed the logic of the renaming of this creature – we presumed that Monsieur Godin should have a capital G.

Later the French authorities introduced a law forbidding the rat traps to be unattended for more than twelve hours and to be inspected every day within two hours of sunrise. The Réglementation contained many more completely unworkable conditions and was typical of laws written by bureaucrats sitting comfortably in their offices in Paris with no knowledge of country ways. Fortunately our local Mayor was a sensible man and turned a blind eye to the more unreasonable requirements.

Sylvestre however managed to choose the introduction of this new law to ask for a pay rise whilst at the same time suggesting that we employed someone else to control the water rats – more for less! Since he undertook none of the other standard duties of an English water keeper such as weed-cutting, fence mending and even collection of the rubbish that somehow always finds its way into the river, we understandably declined. This had the bizarre result that he came even more frequently than before and set the traps daily, despite our agreeing that, given his journey, he could do this twice a week.

Poachers and gypsies (one and the same to him) were, in reality, a great source of delight to Sylvestre. They provided him with an excuse to wave his gun at someone, to threaten them and, once we had him signed up as an official Garde Riviere Assermenté (complete with badge sewn on the camouflage), the possibility to arrest and prosecute them. It may have given him much pleasure but this was always at a cost to us for court papers and so on. We feared increasingly for his safety as he got older for he had a hot temper and was often taking on younger, fitter men who were quite ready to produce a knife. Fortunately he turned gradually to a more subtle approach as he aged and would block in the poachers' vehicle or let down their tyres whilst awaiting the police who often had to come from several villages away to his aid as many of the local stations had closed.

He did however make exceptions. From time to time some poacher appealed to his better nature – usually because they were using a fly rod or because they had made an innocent mistake and strayed onto our stretch by 'error' (passing several signs stating that the fishing was private and climbing over barbed wire fences).

I should add at this point that poachers in France are far more sporting and always seem to fish with a rod and line – what is at the end of this line is another matter – but no huge nets, hand grenades or bleach in the pool here. In these cases he would bring them to the house where we had to pronounce their sentence – this was hugely embarrassing, particularly the first time, as we had no idea what was 'good form'. It turned out that standard practice was to fine them the cost of a fishing licence and give the money to the commune. This apparently feudal system was actually a remarkably sensible way of dealing with the situation. It was important that it be known in the region that we prosecuted poachers '*pour décourager les autres*' (to misquote).

Possibly the most amusing such instance was when Sylvestre, dressed in shorts as he was in all seasons, turned up at the front door with two rather sheepish young men, both with fly rods in hand. It turned out that, not only did they have a valid fishing licence (first good mark, even if it did not allow them access to our private fishing), but also that they had been photographing and filming each catch and then returning the fish to the river. When they saw how the land lay (I was finding it hard to look cross) they volunteered to show me their film and photographs. Whipping out the camera, by this time digital, they showed me their catch on the screen. There before my eyes were the two biggest trout I had ever seen taken from our river – they must each have been 4lbs or more. I could not bring myself to fine these nearly-honest fishermen and settled on them agreeing to send me their photos by email. To my absolute amazement they actually did so and they are in our Fishing Record Book to this day.

To ensure we knew he was doing his job, Sylvestre would knock at the door every time he came, which was daily when we were in residence, and we would have a long, and usually repetitive, conversation about the weather, politics and poachers, usually in that order. His indignation levels rose with the move up the subject scale. This he would do even when it was evident from the cars in the drive that we had a houseful of guests and were in the middle of Sunday lunch. Marthe's uncle had warned us of this trait but it soon became a case of 'it's your turn' as his ancient blue Renault van turned into our gate.

Further Investigation

Leaving the newly-named Stallone to his traps, we returned to the house for a late lunch. As we discussed our morning we thought we could just hear sounds of some creature apparently scuttling across the ceiling just above our heads. Combined with a rather peculiar smell from the larder situated under the stairs which we had put down to damp, we realised that we had a resident – probably also responsible for the noise I had heard in the night. Mice or rats, we assumed, and decided to put down some traps.

It soon occurred to us that our predecessors had never really lived in the house and had cooked entirely with a microwave as there was no oven in the kitchen. As we had no furniture other than one bed that had been left in the house, we resolved to buy the essentials that very day. France is very well served with huge commercial centres where all the basics can be found together. One afternoon sufficed to buy and arrange delivery of all the domestic appliances, plus five beds, towels, sheets and pillows. For the time being we sat on deck chairs and ate off a bridge table that we had brought with us. All this was delivered within two days and all the appliances installed – most efficient.

Asking around, we discovered that there was a huge *brocante – dépot vente* [bric a brac emporos] nearby where over the next few months we spent many a happy hour acquiring most of the furniture we needed, and quite a bit that we didn't. This was mostly very inexpensive, albeit of rustic origin – it did the job.

Two pieces of furniture had been left in the house. The first was a rough sideboard which produced a real bonus in the form of a complete service of Arcopal, a green glassware similar to our Pyrex. Although reminiscent of school, at least we had something to eat off. The back of a large built-in cupboard also coughed up a charming, hand-painted service of plates with a simple sprig design perfectly suited to this farmhouse life.

The second piece was a huge armoir, so large that I doubt it could ever be moved out of the door without total dismantling. Investigation revealed that it contained the few pieces of fishing equipment that the previous owners had deemed of no interest. Oncle Jean's set of drawers for his flies (empty) with a poor carbon copy of a typed list of the flies he had used, each with a brief description of how and when he used them.

This list I later took to Brian at Farlows in London (everyone knows Brian and yet no-one ever seems to use his surname) to try to decipher the list and then to equate the French names to English flies. Traces of Latin in the description helped in this task and we eventually managed to form a fairly comprehensive list for our future use. There were few surprises; most of the classics featured Black Gnat, Wickham's, Greenwell's Glory, BWO and so on. The Mayfly patterns were somewhat different (of which more later) and there were no nymph patterns. One fly I did not know and which I thenceforward adopted with enthusiasm was the Bivisible. The white hackle stands out so well against the second hackle of chestnut brown that this fly is almost always easy to see on the water. I am a great believer that it is every bit as important that the fisherman can see the fly as that the fish can. Without this visibility it seems fairly irrelevant whether you have on the right pattern for the fish's taste.

There was a further surprise in store. A metal cantilevered tool box lay at the bottom of this cupboard and proved to contain a huge collection of miniature spoons, Mepps, spinners, minnows, hooks and Flying Condoms. This must have been Tante Maleine's 'fly box'. It seemed she must have bought a complete new stock every season, such were the numbers. I had never before encountered such armament intended for trout so decided to keep it just so that I could shock my purist friends in the future.

Estate Matters

The next day, after a sleep much disturbed by scrabbling of feet above our heads, we set about deciding how to deal with the rest of our 'estate' consisting of a garden which surrounded the house and one scrubby field, totalling some three and a half acres in total. Having previously rented a weekend cottage back home we knew the pitfalls of too much garden. I had spent every weekend there on the mower, with Marthe weeding, and we had hardly dared to miss a weekend in case the garden got completely on top of us. As this new property had been bought essentially for the fishing, we had no intention of making the same mistake again.

Stallone therefore agreed to undertake the mowing and hedge cutting to start with and we felt we could easily manage the few roses that made up the floral display. We did not plan to plant herbaceous borders or in any way create a lot of work.

Whilst we were wandering round looking at what was to be done, a rather short, solid man of uncertain age with braces holding up his over-sized trousers and with a cigarette glued to his bottom lip approached us and asked, rather diffidently and in a very strong accent, if we had any plans for 'La Cour'. Now I had spent a year studying French at the Foreign Language School in Tours and Marthe is French so you would think we should not have too much trouble understanding anything put to us, even in a strong Norman accent, but this stumped us. There was no courtyard anywhere near – what could he be talking about?

It turned out that he meant the field and he wanted to put his sheep in it to graze. We had not at that stage decided what to do with it but in any case would not be using it ourselves so we decided that the best arrangement would be to allow him to graze the field for nothing on condition that he kept it tidy and cut the hedge annually. This would also get us off on a good footing with the neighbours.

Thus we had the first of our many tenants of La Cour. Some extremely inadequate fencing went up, held together in all ways possible – we soon discovered that this was how the local farmers worked, very much 'make do and mend'. Five rather mangy sheep then duly appeared but over the ensuing months the numbers gradually decreased. Occasionally we saw one on its back with its legs in the air and then it was gone, collected by the sons in their trailer, somewhat furtively. Eventually I could resist no longer and asked what might be wrong with them and was told they had *la maladie des moutons*!

We subsequently discovered that generic diseases were the answer to most things – *la maladie des peupliers* [poplars] was just one other example we later encountered and others followed for alders, elms and so on. In any case there was soon just one sheep left and Monsieur Beaufils, for such was his name, eventually threw up his hands in horror at his sons' incompetence and said we could have back La Cour – but not before we had discovered that his wife was available to work in the house.

Next to take on the field was a quiet, sad faced man who came most days and looked after his sheep with great care. One day he asked if he could 'borrow' an extra little triangle of land out of a corner of our garden. We agreed as it really made very little difference to us. Within a few short weeks he had transformed this triangle into an immaculate vegetable plot, worked to a fine tilth, and soon to produce a myriad selection of herbs and vegetables.

This private man was rightly very proud of his work so we were very surprised on returning the following spring to find the plot had all run to seed and clearly was not being tended. It turned out that, when mowing a lawn for a customer, he had fallen backwards off a bank and had been hospitalised. He never really recovered and he certainly never returned to La Cour. Rumour had it that he had liked a drop to drink.

Next came a man who was to be an important influence on our lives at Cercy. Of truly indeterminate age, Monsieur Lapointe was a squat figure with a pronounced limp and the usual over-large trousers held by braces up to his chest and followed by a mongrel which matched him perfectly in stature; squat, and with an identical limp! This creature turned out to have the splendid name of Urgence.

As we got to know him we learnt that this was a man who lived life by his rules and his alone. He held authority in all its forms in total disdain. Nobody would tell him how he was to do things. We loved to imagine the agents of authority entering his farmyard and endeavouring to enforce some ridiculous law or other. We felt sure that he would see him off his property at the end of his shotgun and with a volley of choice expletives.

Monsieur Lapointe saved horses and ponies of every type and we had seen many of his orphans on the hillside opposite – hence his nick-name between us was always The Pony Man. He now had so many of these unwanted horses, he wanted to use La Cour as an overflow. This, we thought, suited us fine, forgetting of course that horses are highly selective grazers. We then had to insist on his 'topping' the field as part of the agreement to keep the pasture tidy. This he did with good grace and an extremely ancient tractor. Monsieur Lapointe was one of those people who was never going to be called by his Christian name, always Monsieur. It did not make relations any less cordial.

Now we would arrive to the pleasant sight of horses, some near thoroughbred, looking over the fence. This was much more the thing! Monsieur Lapointe was a daily visitor to check on his horses, to keep an eye on the house when we were away and to over-water our geraniums. As with previous tenants of La Cour, no money changed hands but he would regularly bring 'rent' in the form of his local gut-rot Calvados, a huge duck or half a dozen bantam eggs. Occasionally we would return the compliment with a bottle of champagne (which he loved) or whisky. Our little group of local friends was growing.

Our Village

From the day we acquired the property we tried to think of a name for the house, which had no name. Indeed it had the indignity of a number – No 13. How can a country house have a number, even if it is on the edge of a village? (My brother did once live in a cottage in the middle of nowhere and with no neighbours which nonetheless had the address 413 Kilsham Lane. This turned out to be Estate Cottage No 413). Nonetheless the Mayor had given us a blue number plate to put up (25 years later we still haven't done so).

We needed a name so that we could say to our daughters 'We're off to X for the weekend'. Our combined intellect was quite unable to find a name on which we could all settle. We did agree that the best name had been stolen by

Marthe's uncle who had used 'L'Epuisette' for his fishing cabin downstream of us though this turned out to be not inspiration but simply the name of the field on which the cabin had been erected. I was all for 'L'Abreuvoir' (The Trough – as I felt sure that was what it would be when we had lots of friends to stay) but alas this was firmly shot down. To this day we still have to say 'I'm off to Cercy', for we have never found the answer.

Whilst Monsieur Beaufils occupied La Cour we discovered that his wife would be prepared to come and do some cleaning in the house and so she was duly enrolled. Madame Beaufils was a large woman with a florid complexion and hair of a startling shade of red. This varied from time to time, as far as we could tell depending on the colouring on special offer in the local shop.

She was, in brief, energetic but not very thorough. We soon learnt never to ask after her health as she was an expert! She or a member of the family was always unwell and the doctors had always misdiagnosed. She would then, at great length, explain what was really wrong and exactly which medicine was required to put them right. This seems to be at the very least a local, if not a French 'thing'. Everyone is ill, everyone has been misdiagnosed and they all know how to put it right.

She claimed to be able to do anything from the laundry to hairdressing and everything between. One look at her coiffure was sufficient to deter our use of the latter talent. Later a visit to her home was enough to decide us about the former. Not long after Monsieur had removed the last of his sheep, the family upped sticks and moved out of the village. Later we heard plenty of grumbling about the family's nefarious exploits – they never did us any harm but, it appeared, we were lucky.

Cercy is a small, sprawling village of some six hundred inhabitants but sadly the only commerce consists of a junk shop and a pharmacy. The health of the village is very well catered for nowadays as there is a spanking new Medical Centre to provide the pharmacy with clients. Not that the French need much encouragement. Pharmacies in France are unbelievably successful and our little one here has grown from one to three tills in next to no time – not bad for the size of the village.

As for manufacturing, when we arrived there was a brush-making factory but this has closed and is being turned into residences. There is no longer any work to be had in the village which is, essentially, a dormitory town for Rouen.

The beating heart of the village is unquestionably *Chez Arlette*, a Bar Routier. When we first arrived to fish with Oncle Jean this was a run-down, depressing bar with a huge, largely empty car park and no clients. The only vehicles to be seen were a small group of coaches – it was used as the terminus for the local bus service to Rouen. The opening hours were unpredictable and the host unwelcoming – hardly a recipe for success.

Soon however the original owner, the eponymous Arlette, having kept ownership of the bar throughout, returned to take over and in no time at all turned it into a thriving and sought-after eatery. She was always open, most welcoming and served the sort of inexpensive food that one always used to find in Routiers all over France but which have largely disappeared. Furthermore the quality of what was on offer was magnificent for the price – the lorry park was full again.

The extent of Arlette's success was proven when a by-pass was built around the village, taking the traffic away from and above the village and thus further from the river, further enhancing the sense of peace when fishing. Arlette's lorry park however remained as full as ever, proving that if you provide good, simple fare at a sensible price people will '*faire le detour*'.

Arlette herself was the fount of all knowledge. We need a cleaner – 'ask Arlette'. The girl who served in the restaurant over-heard the request and piped up saying that she could do us a few hours when she had finished her shift – thus Sylvie entered our lives and our network expanded again. Her energy put us to shame: the lunch service *Chez Arlette* must have been exhausting in itself yet Sylvie would come on after that and do two or three hours cleaning for us, and always with a wide smile on her face.

As so often the pub is the centre of English village life, so is the Bar Tabac in France. Arlette dispensed cigarettes and knowledge alongside the usual strong coffee and glasses of beer and red wine, apparently regardless of the hour. She also acted as dépôt de pain for one of the local bakeries and so could usually produce an emergency baguette or the occasional croissant.

Our wide circle of contacts grew as we applied to the Mayor for permission to move our entry gate, which he granted without demur, saying that he knew exactly why we wanted to do so. He was right, he did! As we were weekending to start with, we often arrived very late on a Friday only to find our neighbours, or one of their friends, parked across our gate. They never complained at being roused to move, but we felt guilty when it was so late. We also learned from this exercise that the property had never been flooded in living memory, even though the Mayor asked us to allow for a drain to go under our new riverside entrance to continue a centuries-old ditch that ran along the side of the hedge. This despite the fact that it was never seen to hold water. Good news nonetheless, given the increased flooding Europe-wide.

Throughout our time in Cercy we have been lucky to have Monsieur Buchon as Mayor. He has had the good of the village at the front of his mind and has spent his budget wisely – which is no doubt why he was regularly re-elected. We later discovered that he had met his wife and got engaged under what was now our roof – she had been the granddaughter of the then-keeper, Soudet. The secretary to the mayor was his daughter, another source of local knowledge.

One decision Monsieur Buchon took was particularly favourable from our point of view. When we acquired the property the waste water from the village passed through a purification plant situated just upstream of our fishing. Although the water returned to the river was strictly speaking 'clean' we knew from the Hampshire chalkstreams what that really meant. With the best will in the world there was an effect on the quality of the water and hence on the flylife. Nonetheless the river flowed crystal clean to the eye apart of course from the period immediately following a storm when it inevitably coloured up.

Some years later he approached us to ask if he could build a new plant in the water meadows at the top of our beat. He had concluded that the capacity of the current plant would be insufficient for the needs of the village in the near future. We declined the euros waved under our noses. This plan would have meant having a hideous semi-industrial plot situated in plain sight of the house and right alongside the fishing. We would also have had a constant stream of vehicles and people passing right past the house to tend the machinery.

The result of our declining this proposal was that the new plant was built some two kilometres downstream on land belonging to Marthe's uncle. The waste water was pumped all that way down and into the river clear of all our fishing. The old plant was cleared away and nature soon hid all signs that it had ever existed. This was a tremendous result for us and our beat.

One of the driving forces behind the many events in the village is Monsieur Lemarche. He and his wife arrange the annual ceremony for a British pilot who had come down near the village during the Second World War. This touching tradition involves a visit to the crash site just outside the village and, of course, a slap-up meal afterwards, arranged by Arlette naturally. Monsieur Lemarche also runs the small local library which happily accepts all our redundant books and also puts together the old-age pensioners' lunch to which all are invited. He would much rather I did not go, however as he has taken a shine to Marthe and the traditional two kisses on meeting have progressed rapidly through three kisses on the cheek to a wild dive for the lips. He knows I am not an early riser and has taken to early morning calls in the hope of getting Marthe on her own. He is, of course, referred to as her 'boyfriend'. As you will see, I have my 'girlfriend'.

The village also boasts a fish farm and trout hatchery further upstream of us. It straddles both the Andelle and the Echelle and so benefits from a good supply of clean chalk-fed water. It is based around the mill of Bussy and covers a considerable acreage. A dozen or so shallow, concrete, rectangular basins are used for growing on the young troutlets through the various sizes until they reached a saleable size of around three quarters of a pound.

These basins were augmented by three sizeable ponds which had been dug in such a way as to look reasonably naturalistic. Into these ponds are placed some of the larger fish where they are allowed to grow on so that the fish farmer has some substantial specimens to sell on.

He had also contrived a further source of income by allowing visitors to purchase fish at the gate – these were unceremoniously scooped out of the concrete basins with a net and sold per head.

Far more popular however are day or half-day tickets to fish the 'lakes'. At weekends the banks are lined with fishermen (always male) shoulder to shoulder and chucking out ever more outlandish pieces of ironmongery and then furiously reeling them back in. Far from this being an escape from the family, most of these men have brought their wives and children with them. Madame sits in a deckchair happily knitting away as the children play and stray near and far, often with the family dog. A giant barbecue has been provided and regularly emptied bins located all round the lakes complete the 'bucolic' scene.

This peaceful scenario is very occasionally interrupted by one of the fisherman actually hooking a trout, whereupon everyone within sight congregates to watch the battle. Any catch is included in the cost of your day ticket (up to a certain maximum total weight). It is even possible to rent one of these lakes in its entirety, ideal for a corporate day.

With a shop on site selling everything required for fishing and with no need for a fishing permit, it seems the farmer has thought of everything to maximise his income. From our point of view, this much easier fishing can only be good in discouraging the locals from poaching our trout.

The Market Town

If we wanted to buy food, or indeed almost anything, we would have to go further afield. The nearest market town is Ry, a charming place consisting essentially of one main street, a few small side streets and a church dating from the 12th century with an extraordinary carved wood porch. As with most small towns in France there is also a pleasant covered market, though not of any great architectural distinction.

Ry's greatest claim to fame is that it is generally acknowledged to be the inspiration for the village of Yonville in Flaubert's *Madame Bovary*. There is a museum, a Bovary tourist trail and numerous appalling puns in the names of the shops – 'Rêve Ry' 'Le BovaRy'! – there is even a barber's shop with period window display (read the book if you must – I found it unutterably dull).

Looking up the length of the main street, and placed high up to dominate the scene, is an attractive house that we immediately took to be 'The Big House' no doubt owned by the local grandee. Closer inspection showed that it was right on the road that climbed out of the village, not at the end of a long alley of trees, and was one room deep and thus quite small – no manor house this. We later discovered that this is a very typical Norman style of building, the origin or idea behind which we have never discovered.

Market day in Ry is on Saturday which, as we were weekending at the time, was most convenient. When we first started to come on a regular basis this was a fairly extensive affair but it has shrunk somewhat now. Star of the show was without doubt the fishmonger, an ageless woman with wild hair which changed colour every week, always in fiery hues which suited her temperament. She continued to shout out her wares whilst carrying on a running argument with her son who apparently could do no right (though it was always very good-humoured). All the other staples were available with professional stalls for fruit, vegetables and cheese in addition to the fishmonger. There is even a stall, if you can call it that, where a man beautifully re-canes the seats and backs of *bergères* [a type of chair] or replaces the traditional rush seats on dining chairs. He demonstrates his skills whilst awaiting clients

Quite how this tiny town supports four stalls, a greengrocer's shop and a supermarket all selling fruit and vegetables has been a source of mystery to us. One stall drums up business by offering tastings, something rather charming that one finds quite regularly in France, whilst another always slips a little 'extra' into your bag – usually something you really don't want. One young couple run a huge stall with a breath-taking display of everything both in season and out which must take an age to set up. But they always seem to be more expensive than the other greengrocers and their survival is a mystery though they are still there after twenty years so there must be something there.

Meanwhile a motley selection of locals set up their small tables, mostly in the covered market. One of those who stood out was a rosy-cheeked farmer's wife with her hearty produce: potatoes, eggs and whatever green vegetable she happened to have in surplus. She was soon nicknamed 'Mrs Herriot' as she reminded us of that character in the TV adaptation of the wonderful books by James Herriot about his life as a Yorkshire vet.

The second was a miserable-looking, hunched up old lady who sat at her bridge table with a cloth on it and two miserly bunches of wilting parsley. She was quickly named 'Madge' after Dame Edna Everage's down-trodden assistant. We felt sorry for her and nearly always succumbed and bought a bunch until one day a friend spotted that no sooner had she sold a bunch than she sneaked round the corner and produced another from the back of a brand new Mercedes station wagon!

I had a love/hate relationship with the woman behind the cheese counter. She was singularly unfriendly but she had wonderful cheeses, cream sold by the ladle and butter of many types sold by weight and carved off huge pats (no pre-packed items here) – and what a variety! Eventually, after she acknowledged my genuine interest, we struck up some kind of relationship where I could at least get the odd civil word out of her. On one occasion I turned into the covered market and saw to my horror that her trestle tables had all been replaced, bar one, with a refrigerated counter. When I expressed my displeasure at this backward step she explained that she had received a visit from the Health and Safety inspectors who had told her that under Common Market regulations every cheese must be in a chilled counter and that she would be fined per cheese for every cheese not so displayed. When I asked her why she was risking so much when she had a trestle table full of Camembert, Pont l'Evecque, Livarot and Neufchatel outside the cabinet and hence not chilled, she replied with horror that these were Normandy cheeses and she could not bring herself to treat them in such a barbaric way.

These are indeed local cheeses and this is surely the home of the most famous of all French cheeses. We did find however that Neufchatel, unless aged for a considerable time, was a very dull cheese, chalky and salty and not much else. It is however probably the most widely distributed in our region as it is a farm-house cheese needing no special conditions to produce and was available from many of the farm stalls as well as from the specialist.

One market day we were surprised to find that the cheese lady was not set up as usual. Asking around we discovered that she had decided to close down the business as so many people were on diets which excluded dairy products that it no longer made financial sense to continue. As I was on one such health induced diet, I could not fail to understand – but I was sad.

Nowadays the only cheese on the market is a single stall sending hard cheeses from the mountains and not a Normandy cheese in sight. This stall-holder is another who offers irresistible tastings of which I guiltily always avail myself. But what a sign of the times when the home of cheese could no longer support a stall selling this famous product. Indeed one now particularly notices the pretty Norman dairy cattle when seen as they have become increasingly rare, replaced by the ubiquitous Charolais.

There is a local bee-keeper who brings his delicious produce, generally every other week. As a lover of honey myself I quizzed him about the difference between the different honeys he offered. Thus I learnt that there could be a significant variation between honey from the same flowers but from different seasons. The choice is bewildering: honey from acacia, from heather or from 'tous fleurs' and all spring or summer production, not to mention on the comb or in a pot. Of late he has come less frequently bemoaning reduced quantities produced – a familiar cry with the bee under apparent threat Europe-wide.

Ry is fairly self-contained having a butcher, a baker, a very small supermarket, naturally a pharmacy, a ridiculously expensive delicatessen and, rare in France strange to tell, a wine merchant. The latter has become a good friend, as we equally have become a good customer, and he delivers our orders whilst doing the school run (his children are at school in Cercy). No other village in the area supports a wine shop of any description, quite surprising even if Normandy produces no wine. I fear that everyone buys from the supermarkets.

There is a wonderful droguerie selling many a product that would have been known to our great grandparents and which still work better than the modern equivalent. This is run by a manic depressive who takes all the pleasure out of a visit to her emporium by one look at her face alone.

It was in one of the other shops that we witnessed one of the most hilarious scenes we have seen – sadly this will almost certainly not translate to paper but I will do my best. This took place in a small jeweller's shop which sells a few inexpensive items but, above all, mends watches and clocks and replaces batteries and straps. Run by a father and son, it is only open in the mornings as they run the museum of automata which, by deduction, opened in the afternoon. They are, understandably, very proud of this museum as the father had actually made most of the exhibits and kept them all going. This is part of the Bovary tourist trail.

This Saturday morning there was quite a queue – it was market day – but the reason was not hard to find. A stout lady dressed from head to toe in black was negotiating the purchase of a battery-powered alarm clock and the negotiations had clearly already been going on for some time. Marthe rapidly assessed the situation and set off to 'do' the market leaving me to wait my turn. When she returned some considerable time later the performance was still ongoing.

There had been a tremendous thunderstorm in the area the night before and the customer was complaining that her old, mains powered, alarm clock had failed to wake her (because of course all the power in the area had been knocked out by the storm). The conversation went something like this;

Customer: 'Will it wake me up at 7 o'clock?'

Shopkeeper: 'Yes Madame, I can assure you it will wake you up. Of course if you like you can also connect it to the mains power.'

'Will you show me please.'

'First you set it to either the analogue or the 24 hour clock – of course if you choose the analogue clock it will also ring at 7 o'clock in the evening.'

'Yes but will it wake me at 7 o'clock in the morning?'

'I think I should set it for you to the 12 hour clock,' (Fiddles with clock) 'then I set the alarm like this' (Further fiddling).

'Yes but it will wake me at 7 o'clock?'

'Yes Madame, I assure you it will, but I am always here to help you if you have the slightest doubt or problem.'

'But I live 25 kilometres away. I am only here because I am visiting my sister.'

'I can promise you that you will have no problems and I will set it all for you before you go. But please feel free to come back for help at any time.'

'Very well then. Do you have that model in white?'

(Patiently): 'I will have a look Madame' – (Hunts in stock) – 'Yes I do, would you like me to set this for you?'

(Inspects the clock at length): 'No – after all I think I will stick to the black.'

'Right, I will set this one for you.' (Installs batteries and looks mystified) 'Well this is extraordinary! I have never had one of these fail. I will see if I have another one.' (Rummages desperately through stock). 'Well I have one in blue, how do you like that?'

'Will it wake me at 7 o'clock?'

'Yes Madame I promise you it will and I will set it all for you and you know you can always come back if there are any problems.' (Does not wait for an answer and sets the clock and installs batteries). 'There – it's all working now. I will show you how to switch the alarm on and off.' (Demonstrates)

'Excellent!'

'Would you like the box for that?'

'No I don't think I need that really. Just remind me how much that is.'

'That is €28 please.'

(Customer produces a card)

'I am afraid we don't take cards: cash or cheques only.'

'Oh! I am not sure I have that.' (Rummages in handbag. Finally finds chequebook) 'Who do I pay?'

(Shopkeeper having put the clock in a bag) 'Please pay XYZ clocks.'

'Do you know, I think I will have the box after all.'

(Shopkeeper patiently) 'I will have to see if I can find the right one for it.' (Rummages through an enormous pile of assorted boxes and quite remarkably puts his hand straight on the right one) 'There we are.'

'Can I just have another look at the white one.'

(Shopkeeper sighs for the first time) 'Certainly Madame.'

'No, I was right the first time. Let's stick to that.' (Hands over cheque.)

(Shopkeeper hands over the boxed clock) 'There we are. You don't want the instructions do you as I have set it all for you.'

'I think after all I had better have them.'

(Shopkeeper now unpacks the whole thing, inserts instructions, re-boxes the clock and hands it over) 'Now remember Madame that you can bring it back to me at any time for help.'

'Thank you young man.' (This he was not, by any measure.)

As she leaves, the (by now considerable) queue nearly bursts into applause but instead smiles politely.

Not long after this incident we wanted to change a watch strap but found a hand-written note sellotaped to the shop door stating 'Closed due to serious illness'. On asking next door for further information we enquired how serious this illness was only to be told 'Oh he's dead'. A serious case of under-statement.

Bread

The humble *baguette* plays a large role in life here at Cercy. Most French people do not have baguette with every meal and instead will buy *un pain* which is slightly bigger and lasts longer.

In Paris the locals buy *baguettes* because there is a baker at every street corner and so they can easily buy bread twice a day. This is what is required with the *baguette* as it is dry by dinner time if bought for breakfast.

Our English visitors however expect *baguettes* with every meal because that is what they think the French all do – plus of course a *croissant* or a *pain au chocolat*. French visitors like sweet cakes at tea-time. Preferably with lashings of cream – Marthe's 'boyfriend' and his wife devoured two such *petits gateaux* each in the blink of an eye when they called in for tea. Equally popular are the fruit tarts which increase the queues at the baker every

Sunday. I have always found these to be very disappointing, a triumph of appearance over taste.

There is no baker in Cercy. We have a choice either to go to Arlette's bar, which acts as a *dépôt de pain* for the village, or to drive. Recently a third option has entered the running; a machine has been erected in the carpark opposite Arlette's bar dispensing *baguettes*. This is not as ghastly as it sounds – we never considered using it until one day we spotted a baker's van alongside and the baker simply filling the machine with fresh loaves. In our imagination we had assumed it involved some sort of uncooked or half-cooked dough being inserted and then a form of alchemy when money was inserted.

The bread from Arlette varies from day to day as the chosen baker shuts at least once a week and she has to get it from elsewhere. Furthermore she changes supplier from time to time – we do not know the reason or indeed when she has done so. On top of this she by no means always has any croissants.

I am very fussy about my bread and have had flirtations with several bakeries over the years – to the extent that the baker's wife in Vascoeuil was referred to as my girl-friend as I went there so often. She, however, moved on.

The village of Vascoeuil recently was the beneficiary of a considerable legacy from an unmarried resident who died. The mayor decided that, amongst other things, the village needed a bakery again. A clash of wills between him and my departed girl-friend who was trying to sell her shop meant that the fully equipped bakery remained empty and a new bakery was built right opposite. The old bakery is now a hairdresser's shop. Politics, politics.

I transferred my affections to Perriers-sur-Andelle where they have stayed to this day. Certain other bakers pass muster but none match up. Some are banned. I have been known to drive 25 kilometres round to get to Perriers because of a diversion for roadworks rather than suffer bread from elsewhere. I said I was fussy.

Normandy Snippets

One very important task (important to me as I had always wanted one) was undertaken our first season – the erection of a weathervane. No sooner had we bought the house that I had ordered one from a blacksmith in Dorset. My mother had asked what I wanted for Christmas and I was in no doubt – 'as long as you organise it yourself' was her standard response to such requests. There was a forge in the next village to Cercy but, when we visited to ask if they would make us one, they made it clear that they were 'artists' and did not play around with such frivolities.

I resorted to the internet and found a forge that would make to your own design, so I sketched an image of a rising trout and sent it to them. The intricacies involved in designing a weathervane so that it actually works did not occur to me! Somehow they managed to do so whilst, mostly, respecting my drawing. Step forward Stallone to attach it to the little bothy in the garden where it could be seen from the house and still be isolated enough from other buildings to pick up the prevailing wind. An essential fisherman's tool was now in place – funny how it always seemed to point north when the mayfly was up.

A further piscatorial installation came in the form of an early visitor's present. As is my way, I must have said at some point how much I wanted a bell to summon fishermen from the river when the cook had finally lost her legendary patience. Anyhow David Robertson arrived bearing a handsome brass school bell. This was hung with great ceremony from a bracket fixed outside our bedroom window whose original use remains a mystery but which provided the perfect home for our new acquisition. Armed with a long length of rope attached to the clapper and which reached to the ground, this bell can now be heard at the far end of the beat. Fishermen ignore it at their peril as Marthe is very understanding and is a fisherman herself so it is only rung in extremis.

Although definitely on the decline, markets locally still survive, with one within an easy drive of Cercy most days of the week. For the benefit of our visitors we always try to go to the Monday market in Buchy which is quite different to the others. For a start it is on a much bigger scale, though still centred on a splendid 18th century covered market place. The chief attraction however, particularly if there are visiting children, is the large number of locals selling live poultry, rabbits, pigeons and other irresistible wares. No amount of discreet explanation that this box of ducklings is actually intended to end up as food seems to have any effect on children. How we have always managed to escape without a cute cuddly bantam in the back of the car at the very least I shall never know.

I mentioned in a previous chapter a violent local thunderstorm. Buchy is at the head of one of three local valleys – indeed the area is known as Les Trois Vallées – and these thunderstorms tend to follow the line of one or other of these valleys. We can often be sitting in front of our house with the parasol up and a cool drink in hand only to see a storm above the hillside opposite, clearly going up or down the valley of the Crevon without touching us (or indeed the opposite, obviously). These storms seem to be most common during the mayfly season and one is, of course, generally caught at the far end of the beat when they brew up – which tends to happen very suddenly.

Everyone assumes that when you live in France, even part of the year, that you are spoilt for choice when it comes to local cuisine, restaurants and so on. Normandy is not such a place. There is some wonderful local produce, essentially dairy, including some of the most famous cheeses in the world. Apart from that it is apples and everything that can be produced from apples.

Every farm produces their own rough cider and an even rougher calvados which is best used for paint stripping. There is a local travelling still that arrives at each farm and distils their few bottles under licences going back generations. Our own house had had one such licence in the Cartiers' time but it had died with them. I can remember seeing the shining brass of the still – the *'bouilleur de cru'* – parked on the drive, chugging away, and Monsieur Cartier proudly bringing a bottle of his 'calva' with our coffee after lunch. As soon as he was gone Tante Maleine threw her glassful straight on the fire, so rough was the raw spirit. We are still regularly presented with a bottle of this lethal, local brew as a thank you present by a proud farmer – we still don't know what to do with them as drinking is clearly not an option. Some brave friends of our daughters did once try a blind tasting but their heads the next morning precluded any chance of a repeat. The selection of bottles we dare not throw away grows all the time.

Normandy cuisine is a contradiction in terms. In as much as there is any style of cuisine, it is simply that of cooking in or adding cream, cheese or apples (in one form or another). It is unsophisticated cooking. And Normandy produces no wine!

One rather strange thing we have noticed is that virtually all the people with whom we have had dealings, mostly simple farmers, seem to have very well-educated, smart and energetic wives. It has often been some time before we have been allowed to meet them but suspect that in most cases they 'wear the trousers'.

They all appear to be called Françoise.

River Walk

Back now to our first visit after we acquired the stretch of river. It is high time we walk the length of the main branch of our fishing. A stroll of some hundred yards or so along the left-hand bank of the river, of which one branch is right outside our garden gate, brings us to the communal bridge over the Andelle – and the division between the départements of Seine Maritime and l'Eure.

Crossing this substantial bridge (at least it is substantial until the local boys get their hands on it) we immediately cross a tiny stream to our left to enter our stretch. But we enter by the top of the beat so we must hike to the far end before starting to fish. To stay in the good books of the tenant farmer we usually walk down to the bottom of our stretch following the flow of the river whilst staying outside the fence so as not to damage his hay. The way the river is now, this means effectively going round two sides of a triangle. There is however a row of venerable willows which make up, more or less, the third side of the triangle. It has always looked to me as though they trace the line of the river bed at the time of planting. They are much split, as willows do, and regrown from immense trunks which periodically split again.

The custom in the region is to pollard willows annually and no doubt that was how they were originally dealt with until they eventually got out of hand. They are far too big now to consider this approach.

We start where the little run-down hut peeps out from the undergrowth and a forest of huge brambles. This is where I plan to put my first new bench. Upstream there is a good run of streamy, shallow, gravelly water with deeper holes under both banks and opposite is a row of poplars. There are a lot of teasers who rise all day long under the far bank at this point and which prove, if caught, to be sardine-sized despite their sipping rise forms which could suggest a better fish. It is possible to get a fairly long drift without drag along this far bank, given a long cast.

Right alongside the hut there is a large tree overhanging the water beneath which there is a lie which always seems to hold a decent fish. The problem is that the lie is virtually inaccessible without drag setting in as it can only be fished from one position. I eventually gave way to my friends' desperate requests to be allowed to use a nymph at this point and they duly extracted the resident who went just short of 2lbs.

At the top of this stretch an alder sticks out over the river on the point of a slight bend with plenty of shady lairs under its over-hanging roots – but they never seem to produce a fish. Above this is a deeper hole with a large obstruction in the middle. This produces what looks to be the ideal lie for a good fish but actually the fish tend to be slightly further upstream opposite the white bench we come to next. On the other bank is a good stand of mature trees over-hanging the water and this is an excellent reach.

A short barren length leads us up to another S-bend overhung on all sides by trees with exposed roots. There are good fish here but they are extremely hard to attain – the nearest I got was by using a catapult cast with my arms round one of the trees – I still lost the fish. Immediately above the S is a short but excellent fish-producing stretch. There is a dead shrub over-hanging the far bank and it is off this that the best fish can be taken. At this point the main current runs down the far bank bringing all the food to fish lying in that position.

Now we come to a run of some fifty yards or so with mature alders along the whole reach with over-hanging branches, not quite touching the water. If you can cast your fly below these branches, you can generally get a good long float as there is little drag, and have a good chance of a fish. The last tree in this line overhangs a ninety degree bend, with the lowest branch actually trailing in the water. There is always a really good fish lying in this impregnable spot.

After the bend the river opens into a shallower, fast running stretch with a cattle drink opposite and some low shrubs on the far bank leading into the deeper pool described previously. The river has filled in the near bank to the extent it is now firm bank, albeit reedy, in the space of some two or three years. There is a good head of fish in this pool. Another spot for a future bench with views up and downstream.

The far bank is now solidly wooded for a long stretch, round the next bend and up the following straight. The first section is all shallow, rippling water over bright gravel and the lies are all under your own bank.

We then come to another right-angled bend with a long, slow, silty pool with a pronounced back-eddy. The second of the white benches is sited here. The fish in the eddy (and there is always one) has to be approached and fished from the upstream position as the current will bring the fly back upstream to him. He can be caught (and he and his successors have been).

Ignore the following long, dark straight stretch with a strong current; there are hardly any fish in it and those that are, are small. But this leads into a left-handed bend with scrubby alders along the far bank. Fish rise here all the time, even when there is nothing doing anywhere else on the river. From here to the end of the next pool we do not own the opposite bank but worry not, we have only once seen anyone fishing it. I am planning another bench here at what is Marthe's favourite spot. It has produced some decent fish.

A short, shallow run leads from here into the deepest pool on the river. Here too the current hugs the far bank from the head to the tail of this pool and there is a deep, slow current under your bank – do not waste your time there. Concentrate on the fast water at the head of the pool and then below the largest trees on the far bank. You will notice throughout that there are very few trees on the right-hand bank from which we fish – no fools, our predecessors.

Another fast, barren run, and then we are into another, gentle bend with really good holding water under your bank, turning into the run for home. A bench is well situated above this with panoramic views of the river up and down stream.

From here it is more or less a straight run to the bridge which is our home straight. A number of leats drain the fields on your bank into this stretch, so watch where you walk, though there are the remains of plank bridges to assist, albeit very ancient and somewhat decrepit. The whole stretch is good with varied water depths, good eddies and curls, just the right number of obstructions and holding places the whole way. This is a very productive part of the fishery.

Finally there is the pool under the bridge. There is a cattle drink on each side of the river here and to fish this pool you have to stand in one. The fish lie under the left-hand bank just below the bridge. They also move well out into the current when they are on the feed. Therefore you need to side-cast your fly up under the bridge so that it is already fishing before it comes out of the shadow of the bridge.

What had we Bought?

We had a stretch of chalkstream. We knew it used to hold a good head of wild brownies. Did it still? We needed to find out where we stood so that we could plan for the future and establish how to maintain and then improve the fishing from every angle.

With natural excitement at our purchase we were keen to get friends over to fish. However the mayfly, which would have given us our best chance to see the stock levels, was over for the year. That unique insect, being so much larger than most on offer to the trout, tends to persuade even the reluctant risers to come to the surface for the scant few weeks that it appears.

Having therefore very little idea of stocks, and fearful at the numbers that Oncle Jean took out in his time, I decided to set out some basic rules to ensure that we did not further reduce numbers. In brief our first guests were asked to fish upstream dry fly only (no nymphs – rather mean of me as I have always been somewhat incompetent with the nymph), no wading and to return any fish not required for the pot, unless bleeding. In any case no fish above 1½ lbs to be taken as we had no idea if there were any sizeable trout still in residence. My memories of fishing with Oncle Jean, and the records in my fishing book, were that the average was around ¾ lb and that there were few fish above 1½ lbs.

The only exception to the 'no wading' rule so far given has been to allow a young friend to practise the Japanese art of Tenkara which necessitates wading as it involves a long rod and a very short line and a method not dissimilar to dapping. He has been successful but not noticeably so. His letter of thanks included an imprint of a fish he had caught here made using a Japanese method of covering the fish with ink and rolling it on hand-made paper (as far as I remember it). The result is most attractive.

We did have the great advantage of knowing the two similar beats a little downstream owned by Marthe's uncle and aunt respectively and to which we could compare our situation. These had each been treated quite differently and with widely differing results.

All three stretches had in common that they were never let to outsiders and thus the fishing pressure had been light. The beat immediately below our lowest stretch had been fished fairly regularly by family and friends, though chiefly weekends only and mainly during the mayfly. The rule here was, again, that all fish be returned unless required for the pot. Average size was greater than on our stretch, though the river was a little wider here, but the beat was regularly stocked with fish of a reasonable size. A brief recce appeared to show that fish density was noticeably less than ours.

Tante Odette who owned the third beat a few kilometres downstream was by now 'of a certain age' and no longer had many visiting rods and so pressure here was very light indeed. The river this far down was considerably larger and also split into two branches over much of its length. The fish were considerably larger, as our only experience of fishing it showed, with the average of the fish we caught not far short of 2 lbs. However numbers were dramatically down on its heyday and now they were few and far between.

Tante Odette, as she was universally known, was a great beauty and acted as ambassador for the well-known champagne house Pol Roger, in which role she was widely known. She was the great grand-daughter of Sir Richard Wallace, who bequeathed Hertford House in London and its wonderful contents to the nation and, with her two sisters became known as 'The Wallace Collection'.

She had entertained a great deal in earlier years, with visitors representing the 'great and the good' of many worlds. Diplomats, politicians, soldiers, the *'beau monde'* as well as the wine trade of course, all found their way to St Pol, her charming and perfect château in miniature on the banks of the river. She was a great friend of Winston

Churchill who may well have fished here, as certainly did Charles Ritz, son of the founder of the eponymous hotel chain and a famed fisherman and author. He writes fondly of the Andelle in his autobiography *A Fly Fisher's Life*.

Stories about her are legion, and many apocryphal, and include a description of her returning from a dinner in a full length ball-gown and upon alighting from her car (usually a Bentley in the stories, although she never owned one) she spots a trout rising, tucks her gown into the top of some hastily acquired waders, strides down to the river and catches it – first cast of course. Stallone, who was keeper for all three properties, no doubt did much to embellish these stories.

Her property, apart from the river described above, consisted of the aforementioned château in miniature, complete with round, spired tower. In the considerable grounds was a walled garden put down to vegetables and, even more so, to flowers to cut for the house. On our one and only visit we were encouraged to help ourselves and came away with arms full of glorious scented, old-fashioned roses. Sadly, by the time we had acquired our river beat, she seldom came to enjoy them.

Did all this contradictory information really help? First to find out what our own stocks were like.

Early Sorties

In the end, the first year provided few opportunities for fishing, with all our time taken up with making the house habitable. Nonetheless we did manage to get down to the river for the evening rise on a few occasion, with very indifferent results, despite the surface showing that we still had plenty of fish. Our limited experience had not suggested to us at that stage that the rises we were seeing were more than likely to sedges, so our baskets remained resolutely empty.

It was to be the following season before we could draw any significant conclusions on stock and size levels. We invited some of our keen fishing friends and started to catch some fish, of which there seemed to be plenty. The average still seemed to be around the ¾ lb mark, as it had been when we had first fished with Oncle Jean. We decided to stick to my 'rules' set out at the start and to give it a couple of years before deciding on any changes needed. Nonetheless we caught some sixty fish that season (1997) and took out around twenty. All this with very light fishing, weekends only, averaging three rods and with a concentration on mayfly time when invitations were accepted with alacrity. At this stage, I was still working full time and thus we were not able to cross every weekend. A successful first year.

We soon realised that most fishermen were struggling with the speed with which these wild fish were rejecting the artificial, despite my briefing including an instruction that 'you cannot strike too soon'.

This year did however produce our first significant fish and it went against everything I have just said. Our niece, Savine, who had never fished before and was 'under instruction' at the time, had briefly been left to her own devices whilst I went to supervise another youngster.

I came round the bend to see her lighting a cigarette with the rod tucked under her arm, the line trailing in the water. Whilst I watched, a fish rose to her fly, which was awash, turned and hooked itself (no quick strike here). 'Strike', I yelled which had the effect of making her jump out of her skin more than anything else. Eventually I persuaded her to raise the rod tip and, remarkably the fish was on! We managed to bring it to the net and we found we had our first 2lb fish – her first ever. Not bad for a wild brownie and by some way the biggest to date. It is surprising how many fish are caught in such unlikely ways as we have had catches made when the fortunate 'fisherman' was unwrapping a boiled sweet, inspecting the fly-box and so on. Everything bar the right way!

1998 showed catches increase to 85 fish with 30-odd taken out but with signs of a slight decrease in the average size and no sizeable fish landed. This trend continued over the next two years, though numbers held up well, and encouraged a change in our instruction to rods. We felt that the lowering average might be due to larger fish turning cannibal and not only eating the smaller fish but also becoming chiefly bottom feeders and shy to rise to the fly except during the mayfly. We decided to take out any fish of 1½lbs or more as well as any needed for the kitchen. All fish shorter than the cork handle of the rod to be returned, unless bleeding. Still no wading (there really is no need here) or nymphing.

This change began to pay dividends with the average increasing and larger individual fish beginning to be caught once more. After Savine's 2lb fish the first year, it was ten years before we had another, but then they became a regular occurrence. Maybe we were on the right track.

Everyone likes reassurance and I am no exception. We therefore invited a friend of my brother who owned a magnificent stretch of the Itchen at Martyr Worthy, to come and fish and at the same time give us his assessment of the current state of the river and any advice for improvement. Given the quality of his own beat, which I had fished, I shall never forget his opinion that the river was in great 'heart' and that he had never seen all the 'good' weeds growing together in the same place. Praise indeed. He also gave some advice, not the least of which was the need to fence the bank for the whole length to protect from the ravages of the combined efforts of water rats and the cattle. He had indeed fenced the whole of his own beat, to great effect. He also suggested areas where the banks could be strengthened and the current re-directed to scour out areas of silt or further protect crumbling banks. Some of these measures we were to undertake at a later date.

It was clear that, in common with most rivers in the UK, the flylife was in overall decline and fewer fish were feeding on the surface. This was a problem that was going to be hard to solve, the chief challenge being the chemicals used by the farmers finding their way into the river. Some rivers were experimenting with fly-boards suspended from bridges, but we were not yet ready for that.

Dissection of catches revealed the presence of healthy stocks of freshwater shrimps. Indeed we found out subsequently that any log that remained in one place for any length of time would, if turned over, reveal huge numbers of these creatures. The flesh of the trout was as pink as salmon as a result.

Talking to Stallone confirmed what we had seen (or rather not seen): that there were no coarse fish at all in this stretch of the Andelle apart from the very occasional pike. We have never to this day seen a pike in our stretch but Stallone calls on us at the start of every season and tells us that he thinks he has seen a pike in the 'Trou de Bombe' – this is a very deep, slow pool reputed to have been created by a second world war bomber either overshooting Rouen (a bad miss) or (more likely) dumping the remainder of his load before turning for home. Stallone then encourages us to spin this pool with various Rapalas that he produces in order to remove this fictitious pest. At the beginning we used to give it a go but now we just nod sagely. Actually we think it should be part of his job!

Equally there are no grayling – just trout. There is the very occasional rainbow trout taken but essentially just brownies. The rainbows are almost certainly escapees from the fish farm up at the top of the village. This may be the source of a future mystery catch – but that is another story.

A Mystery Sorted

One of the improvements to make in the house was the need to get an uninterrupted night's sleep! The scrabblings from above our heads had gone from bad to worse and could now be heard inside the wall between two bedrooms and directly above our bed. They generally started around two o'clock in the morning and were now accompanied by high-pitched squeaking. Our traps had remained resolutely empty and we were at our wits' end. Send for Stallone!

A brief description of our problems elicited the information that this was, of course, a *fouine*, probably with a brood of youngsters. The faithful Larousse showed to our immense surprise that a *fouine* was a pine marten. Whilst pretty rare in the UK they are apparently pretty common in France and their preferred residence is the lofts of houses, particularly second homes like ours where they can spend the winter undisturbed.

What to do? These creatures are roughly the size of a cat so were unlikely to be taken in a mouse-trap. Furthermore Stallone told us that they were protected under French law as at home.

'Leave it to me,' he said. 'I will prepare them an omelette'. This proved to be some eggs injected with strychnine. It also proved to be very efficient which was a great relief. Sad though it is to kill a wild animal, living with them had proved impossible. The effect of the 'omelette' is to make the martens very thirsty and they will generally go down to the river and expire there. Two of our later such visitors, however, never made it out of the building and were found dead in the stable. We were at least therefore able to see what we had been up against. It is extraordinary to imagine that such a large creature can squeeze through the tiny openings via which they had attained the loft. I have subsequently discovered that there are attempts being made to reintroduce this creature in Wales – good luck!

Anyone who has not experienced living with these animals cannot possibly imagine what they put you through. There is a scene in a popular French film *Les Petits Mouchoirs* (*Little White Lies* is the English title) where the lead character is driven to extreme measures to rid himself of his resident *fouine*, taking a sledge-hammer to the walls and, essentially, having a nervous break-down. Without knowing what I know now, I would have thought this scene to be completely ridiculous – I no longer do.

For the time being we were free of this pest but we were to have further visitations later on. Clearly the sign had gone up stating 'Comfortable family residence with vacant possession'. Stallone was very successful at getting rid of them once they had taken up residence but was there a way of preventing them coming in the first place? We asked around and, in the way of country folk, Monsieur Lapointe had an infallible solution. He told us to scatter moth balls all around the likely areas and possible entry points and we would see them no more. It sounded like an old wives' tale but to date it has continued to work. Our concern is that, in their wisdom, the EU has now banned the sale of moth balls and our stocks are running low. Equally Stallone's stock of, strictly illegal, strychnine is also running low.

Although they could not be described as a pest, we were also at this time plagued by bees. They caused us no real problems as no one was stung, but we worked out that their nest was situated between the floorboards of our bedroom and the ceiling of the kitchen. We were warned that if the bees were left to their own devices the honey would eventually seep out of the nest and through the ceiling. We thus decided to rid ourselves of this problem and called the fire brigade – the first port of call in France for such incidences. Their solution was to spray them with cans that we could have bought in any local shop. This, rather unsurprisingly, had no effect apart from annoying the previously calm bees.

We were then directed to local bee keepers who were delighted to take the swarm off our hands. Their method of doing so was fascinating. They erected a scaffold outside the bedroom window and over a period of several days gradually attracted the bees into a hive placed on the scaffold tower. When this was complete they lifted the floorboards of the bedroom to clear out the nest which turned out to be already of considerable size and, with nothing to contain it, would have spread indefinitely. This had been a good decision.

Further River Ramblings

It was clear that we had some work to do to repair the banks and improve the infrastructure – bridges, benches and so on. However, whilst the cattle could access the river, any such work would be a complete waste of our time and money. Therefore we took the plunge and decided to fence the whole stretch on both banks – where we owned the bank. Stallone received his orders and set to with a will. As with everything he did, the result was immaculate (and very expensive). At least we felt it would last.

He had installed at intervals in the four-strand barbed wire fence six 'Norfolk' gates along the right-hand bank. These are variously called 'Hampshire' gates etc depending on where you are in the world – perhaps they should be 'Normandy' gates here? These gave us easy access at most of the right points as they can be opened and shut with one hand only which is useful when carrying a rod. Bizarrely he failed to put one at the very bottom of the beat, exactly where most people want to start.

We were delighted to see the back of the cattle when fishing. Of recent times the farmer had tended to put bullocks in the water meadows rather than the placid dairy cattle of previous years and they took great delight in charging the fishermen. Even though they would stop if challenged with much shouting and waving, we were never totally at ease.

Contrarily they would also sometimes creep up on you from behind when your concentration was all on a rising trout. Many was the time I felt the breath of a bullock on the back of my neck followed by a nudge on the shoulder which made me jump out of my skin. We accepted the required changes in our casting action as a fair exchange for the absence of bullocks and the improvement to the banks. There was a good deal of cursing and a fair number of lost flies whilst getting used to the barbed wire, but it was worth it.

Drinking places were provided for the cattle on both sides of the river. Our purchase contract required us to provide water for the cattle but did not express how – we could have arranged for a trough had we so chosen. The flaw in this otherwise perfect arrangement was the very short stretch of the left bank that we did not own. For this we required the farmer, Monsieur Coligny (who sub-let the pasture from Monsieur Dumont, son of the farmer from Oncle Jean's time – an illegal and highly unsatisfactory arrangement) to provide a short length of electric fence without which all our fencing would be in vain. We manage to track down the lawyer in Rouen who owned this short (but annoying) stretch of the left bank and sought his permission to fence it, which he gave willingly – as I have said previously he and his family never came to fish anyway.

We telephoned Coligny and asked for a meeting. Amidst endless assurances and sage nodding of the head, he undertook to put up this short length of electric fencing before letting his cattle out to grass in the autumn. The dairy cattle that had previously grazed the meadows on either side of the river had been less of a problem under the care of Monsieur Dumont père, as the fences were in good repair, dividing up the pasture which was used in rotation, with the herd being taken in twice a day for milking. Thus pressure on any particular part of the river was limited.

These had now been replaced by Coligny with Charolais which had free run over the entire acreage as the fences had been allowed to run to rack and ruin. Furthermore these heavy cattle were capable of simply flattening a fence if they took it into their heads to do so. The state of the fencing separating the various *parcelles* was now deplorable and the meadows were becoming over-run with thistles and nettles. The son was not the father and his tenant was even worse.

By this time I was considerably less mobile and was having difficulty getting down to the river from the main commune bridge. Stallone was once more called in to do what he liked best (after persecuting poachers). Access to the river involved crossing a little side stream (which joined the L'Echelle to the main river and was lovely gravelly spawning water) and then descending some two feet or so. We explained what we needed and left him to do it in the off season.

Come Easter the following year we returned to very contrasting results. The farmer had failed to maintain his flimsy electric fence which the cattle had completely destroyed, including the generator and battery. They had then crossed the river and trampled up and down the length of our beat, unable to get out on that side because of our new fence and too stupid to return. The devastation thus left rendered us speechless. Knowing we had to stay on good terms with the locals as absentee landlords, had to be balanced against our attempts to improve the fishing, which the farmers failed to comprehend.

By contrast Stallone had built what was soon christened 'Le Pont Neuf' by my old friend John Stevenson. It was certainly built well enough to stand as long as its namesake in Paris. With oak planks of impressive thickness, beautifully wrapped in chicken wire to avoid slipping, furnished with a tubular steel hand-rail and its own Norfolk gate, the new bridge was a thing of beauty. Since then he has built 'Le Pont de Tancarville' an even more impressive structure of great length and built to see out our grandchildren. This replaced the bridge known and marked on our river map as 'Plunkett Plank', broken as it was when crossed by said Peter Plunkett.

One good thing to come from the fencing of the banks was the rapid recovery of the river-side flora. Kingcups, ragged robin and wild iris were soon appearing in many places and greatly improved the appearance of the stretch. Wild flowers had, in general, been largely absent previously as the cattle had grazed right to the water's edge. The only flowers to be seen before had been the ubiquitous may blossom and one solitary dog rose which was presumably unpalatable to the cows and flourishes to this day.

The fishing continued to improve nonetheless and we were now confident enough in the quality to invite some of our keen fishing friends to come and improve the catch. The mayfly hatches were spectacular with the water meadows submerged in clouds of 'dancing' insects. One peculiarity was that, despite this, we saw remarkably few mayfly spinners on the water – we have never discovered why.

This reminds me of a question which has always exercised me – why is it that the wind during the mayfly always blows downstream? This does not only apply on the Andelle (northerly) but seems to apply everywhere. Given that the fly in use is generally a winged pattern with a very large surface area, the effect is that of trying to cast a helicopter into the wind with resultant knots, kinks, curses and so on. Thank goodness chalkstreams have a tendency to gradually alter their direction ending up, in some cases, with such serpentine curves that you can be casting back to back with someone who is half a mile downstream. This habit means that despite this spiteful May wind one can usually find a corner where the wind is in your favour.

So when is the mayfly season on the Andelle? I believe it to be very similar to the south of England – indeed we find that the climate as a whole is virtually identical in Normandy, just a few days behind. A few mayfly can be seen from around 10th May but it takes the fish time to wake up to the fact that these really are food, and as the Michelin Guide would say, *'vaut le détour'* – a large enough creature to be well worth putting in a bit of extra effort to catch.

As a result the trout seem to be properly 'on' the fly by 17th of the month and it carries on well into June. Indeed, the first weekend in June had historically been considered the best, though now I would say that was a bit late for the very best fishing and that the rise is beginning to tail off. Unlike some rivers I have fished which have a trickle of mayfly through to August, our cut-off is fairly sharp and seldom do we see one beyond the end of June.

I am reminded by this of one of the most magic moments I have encountered beside a river. I was fishing the Wissey, a chalkstream in Norfolk, with Tim Bridge. It was a blazing hot day in August and as I idly followed the passage of a natural mayfly float unmolested for a long distance downstream, I heard the wonderfully moving final act of 'Tosca' floating clearly across the river to where I lay smoking a pipe. I had not realised there was a house opposite as it was only visible from further downstream and the whole incident was faeric.

We also had many a frustrating evening rise at Cercy with the rings of rising fish everywhere but with very poor returns – not an uncommon occurrence. Why is it that, when the fish are rising freely like this, one cannot concentrate on one fish and must, instead, rush from one fish to the next – catching none? It is a little like the difficulty of persuading oneself to pick one partridge out of a covey and to pull a bead on that bird rather than, as one is inclined to, blindly shooting into the midst of the whole covey.

By the time one has decided to stick to one fish it is too dark to see to change the fly and one ends up fishing towards the moonlight shining on the river in order to be able to see the silhouette of your fly on the water and using whatever is currently tied on. This is seldom a recipe for success.

The recompense for staying out late is the glorious return from the river on a balmy summer's evening with the bats just starting to hawk over the river and seeing the lovely, soft, yellow light shining from the windows of the house and maybe a curl of wood-smoke from the chimney – a very welcoming sight as you tramp home for a welcoming glass of whisky. Even in August a fire is often needed at the end of the day as the house remains cool throughout and the afternoon sun does not have the power of earlier in the year to warm the house. Indeed we light a fire most days, apart from the height of summer in July.

This view encouraged another improvement. Our house, although close to the river, is on the edge of the village and I always felt that this idyllic scene was somewhat spoilt by the ugly modern houses for which planning permission had been granted and which could be seen behind our farmhouse on the return from fishing. Having allowed the hedges of La Cour to grow higher, we then decided to plant trees along our borders to further hide these monstrosities (not the least of which was the Medical Centre). To date we have planted a grove of silver birches in La Cour and various ornamental trees in the garden. Things are improving.

More Fishy Things

One evening spent with Tim, when the second decanter of port was circulating, we decided that the best pools and runs on the beat needed names. This was now more necessary as I had become fairly immobile and I loved to hear the reports of the returning fishermen and to know where they had caught (or lost) fish or seen something of interest. I was now fishing vicariously.

We started by deciding that every good beat we knew elsewhere had a Fence Pool, a Bridge Pool, a Rock Pool and so on and, as the evening drew on, introduced some of our more unusual names – Amen Corner (inspired by Augusta National golf course's famous run of holes where many dreams are sunk) and the VW pool which was named after a large rock (we think) in the middle of the river and which resembled a sunken Volkswagen Beetle. Our efforts can be seen on the map on page 7 of this book so you can judge for yourselves how well we did. Trust me, there is a story behind most of them.

At Laird's Cast (my favourite bench is placed here – a great place to view a good length of river, looking upstream and the ideal place to smoke a pipe whilst awaiting the first rise on a hot summer's day), another visitor, Nick James, caught a very small fish which he reported was a salmon parr. Salmon have never been known to run the Andelle though seatrout have been caught as far up as Fleury-sur-Andelle, a few kilometres downstream of us. But Nick is a very experienced fisherman and would know a salmon parr from a troutlet.

Stallone of course said this was nonsense and flatly refused to believe it. Some months later however he had to eat his words as during one of his interminable daily visits he produced the local paper in which was published an article, illustrated with a photo of a salmon parr, which stated that when electro fishing downstream, seven parr had been stunned and netted out for inspection. Stallone is a countryman through and through but his knowledge of all things fishing falls well short of what he imagines it is. He is a keen shot but no fisherman.

There is nonetheless a somewhat more prosaic possible explanation to this catch. As previously mentioned there is a fish farm on the other side of the village and on one occasion we noticed a sign announcing that this weekend's attraction was a *Journée Saumon*! The only way this was possible was to temporarily import some salmon. Could that be the cause eventually? I confess that I think this unlikely and much prefer the thought that one day we will be landing a 20 lb salmon from the Andelle.

I love eels! I particularly love smoked eels. Whilst we have never actually seen eels here, they must be passing through as, almost on demand, Stallone will produce a basket of live eels which he catches a little downstream. I have a hot-smoker in which I have treated many of our trout as I prefer the taste of trout when smoked. This would do the job. My brother, who is in the forestry business, when asked for a few oak chippings for this machine, produced a bag of such dimensions that I doubt we will ever come to the bottom of it, given that the average dose is five tablespoons.

Faced with my first basket of eels however I was at a loss. How did you kill these things? Tante Maleine had always seized them behind the head with a tea towel and chopped off the head. I tried. I tried again. I failed. Faced with total failure I asked Stallone who recommended putting them in the fridge overnight and repeating the exercise. This I did, putting the whole basket in a plastic bag which wriggled most of the night. As soon as they felt the warmth of my hand the next day they came back to life and I failed again.

Not wishing to admit defeat I took the idea to its logical conclusion and put them in the freezer. Finally I had some compliant eels – and delicious they were, smoked and served with horseradish sauce.

French Rules & Red Tape

The dates of the official fishing season on the Andelle are set by the official Federation Departementale etc etc (very long French bureaucratic title). It runs from the second Saturday in March to the third Sunday in September. These dates are specific to rivers of 1 ère Categorie (first class) and rivers of lesser quality have slightly different dates.

There is a generally ignored rule that fishing must cease at nightfall. In our case this rule, if applied, would prevent what is often the best part of the fishing day. This is the result of our stretch being backed by a hill of some size behind which the sun dips long before 'true' nightfall. Further, as the river runs more or less north-south, the sun is behind the fisherman most of the afternoon and the effect of the lengthening shadows naturally becomes more and more of a problem as evening draws in until this hill comes to our rescue.

Minimum take length is 30cms and the maximum basket per head is three per day. Again I am afraid these rules are largely ignored and we set our own, as previously mentioned. As to methods of capture it seems that 'anything goes' apart from fish roe and worms (on 1ère Categorie rivers). Needless to say we once more set our own rules. I rely on my friends not to fish with worm or roe without my having to tell them!

Licences are available for various periods from a single day upwards and can be purchased on-line. This sounded wonderful. The reality is somewhat different. The website simply does not work and takes the applicant on a circular ride back to where he started without actually achieving his aim.

We have therefore always bought our Cartes de Pêche the old fashioned way – from a shop. This however has proved almost as difficult. No sooner have we found a shop that sells them than it closes down. This has taken us from a sports shop in Charleval to another sports shop in Ry, back to a new owner of the shop in Charleval then to the retired hairdresser in Cercy (selling them from home) back to a Bar Tabac in Charleval and so on. This is surely dedication to upholding the law but, as owners of the fishing, we feel obliged to keep on the right side even if our visiting rods are not always so law-abiding.

As on many rivers we are occasionally visited by that pest, the canoeist. The law states that we cannot prevent their use of the river as long as they never set foot on the bed of the river. Their passage cannot be prevented by any means. The farmers ignore this completely, stretching strands of barbed wire across the river to prevent their cattle from straying up or downstream. These strands are set at precisely canoeist's head level – whether by design or coincidence I cannot say.

We have not discovered what the rules are on the subject of swimming – this being France there must be some, if only so that they can be ignored. Given the constant low temperature of chalkstreams (usually around 10°C) you would be forgiven for doubting that anyone would want to swim. Marthe and our daughters did try during one very prolonged spell of hot weather but they didn't stay in long.

But the locals do occasionally give it a go. Fortunately they tend to stick mostly to the public water upstream but the lure of 'bombing' the Bridge Pool can prove too much. A quiet word is usually sufficient.

The Road Beat

There has always been enough water to fish without ever really investigating the two other stretches that we had also inadvertently acquired. However, as time went by and our visitors came for the second or third time, we decided it was time to see what they were made of.

The first we looked at was the downstream beat which ended at the bridge carrying the Route Nationale over the river. Access was a challenge in several ways. It was too far to walk from the house without wasting too much valuable fishing time and so involved taking the car – this to me immediately put it at a disadvantage as one of the charms of our main beat was that it was a gentle meander from the house and so one could go fishing 'at the drop of a hat'. Then you had to park the car – on the grass verge of a very busy Route Nationale! Whether this was legal I have never discovered but the poachers did it too so I never looked into the matter. It is true that we were frequently 'flashed' by passing cars suggesting that maybe it was not.

Once out of the car and equipped with rods and so on, one had to get over a very rusty, high and rickety iron gate and from there onto a flight of three enormously high concrete steps which led down into a thicket of nettles which were more or less up to eye level. If you got to the other side with all your equipment intact it was a triumph. More often than not I found myself searching for my landing net in the nettles.

This escapade brought you out at the bottom of the beat and so you could start fishing immediately. The pool in front of you could only be fished on a dead drift, letting out a huge amount of slack to pick up the cross currents as the fly drifted beyond you downstream. There was no room to stand stream-side of the jungle crossed to access the river and the water was too deep to wade (even if I had not forbidden wading). It was evident though that this pool was heavily poached, festoons of nylon hanging from trees on both banks and the grass well flattened along the near bank. Being accessible from the bridge made this pool a natural target (and as long as the fisherman stayed on the bridge he was not actually poaching) and I doubt there is ever much left in it.

Moving swiftly on you come to a long, straight stretch of pretty shallow, rippling water over a clean gravel bed. For the whole of this stretch we only owned the right bank, but this was no problem as the far bank was so heavily wooded as to be unfishable for its whole length. This was dotted with occasional alders which we kept at a manageable size by annual lopping – until, that is, one year disaster struck!

Stallone arrived at the house all a'fluster one morning and told us that he had caught a contractor cutting down all the trees along our bank of this stretch. He had asked under whose orders this was been carried out and had assured the workmen that they had been misdirected and ordered them to stop immediately.

By the time we got there it was too late and the whole beat had been cleared of every tree and bush. Much correspondence followed but we finally accepted that the alders would soon re-claim their territory and that it was simply not worth pursuing an action through the courts.

This reach has proved remarkably unproductive to date – we shall see what happens now the banks have been cleared. As expected the alders are well on their way to recovery and will very soon need their annual haircut.

At the top of the reach was a deep, slow pool on an almost right-angled bend overhung by some substantial trees on both sides (before the disaster). This pool proved the only really productive part of the whole stretch. It was rare to return from a trip to this beat empty-handed even though the pool was hard to fish with several, subtle cross currents that were hard to see and drag often set in before they had been identified. If a fish was deceived into taking a fly here it was often a good one. The loss of the mature trees may have more of a negative effect than the removal of the alders – only time will tell.

Standing above these trees on the bend, a very long cast was required to reach the one or two tempting risers under the far bank, just above our boundary. Fish here were subjected to even lower fishing pressure than elsewhere, unless one counts the poachers who, judging by the patches of trampled bankside herbiage, were pretty active. I may be being a little unkind as some of these patches could have been caused by wild boar coming down from the forest to drink, which was very close at this point, as we knew they did even though we never saw them.

Given that we have not fished this beat very often and that the farmer generally now just takes a couple of crops of hay off the field and no longer puts bulls to graze as he did before, we have never considered it necessary to fence it off and the banks remain sound. For some reason I have never seen a water rat on this beat.

The Ditch

I have previously described the Echelle, the stretch running parallel to the road and which resembles a carrier. We came across some old photos in the armoir and amongst them was one of a man that Marthe recognised as her great-uncle, fishing with his 'man' standing behind him with the landing net. The stretch they were fishing was unmistakably the Echelle. If it was worth their while fishing it when they had the whole river to themselves, perhaps it was worth a look. It was no larger in the photograph than it was now so we decided to give it a look.

My own first recce revealed only that it was going to be very hard to fish and I only saw very small fish which all spooked immediately – it was hard to approach unseen except crawling, Red Indian style. My report merely 'egged on' our guests who became extremely competitive over this tiny strip of water. This competition grew stronger when Patrick Steuart-Fotheringham pulled out a fish just short of 2lbs!

Aware there was at least one more decent fish still in there, Tim Bridge trumped Patrick with a fish going on 2½ lbs after his departure. An email was duly sent with an attached photograph – 'Patrick, where were you?' From those early successes, The Ditch, as named by Tim, has become a prime beat and possession was much disputed. It has never failed to produce a good fish each year since and its best to date is just over 3lbs, an astonishing size for such a tiny piece of water. These good fish have only ever been taken during the mayfly and generally, though not always, on an artificial Mayfly.

Watching these fish however, it is clear that they have the place to themselves, cruising virtually the whole length of The Ditch and eating the whole way – probably eating their nephews, nieces, brothers and sisters too.

The Ditch, difficult as it is to fish, nonetheless has its devotees, chief amongst whom are Tim and my cousin Henry Mallory. Henry is so dedicated to it that when it became overgrown, he arrived with loppers and his chainsaw in the back of the car and spent a very long, hot day clearing some substantial trees and branches to make it vaguely fishable once more.

It was after this visit that Patrick created the Croisy Killer, an artificial Mayfly based on his observations on the Andelle. Patrick is a superb fly dresser and attached his first examples to his thank you letter on his return home. It has lived up to its name and I have had several dozen tied up by a professional to give as gifts to visiting rods. This fly has yellow wings which, interestingly, is a characteristic shared by the few artificials available in the local tackle shops. To the naked eye the mayfly here does not generally appear any more yellow than elsewhere. Patrick must have seen something, as had the local dressers, because the fish like it and it fully lives up to its name.

The full pattern for the Croisy Killer is:

Hook: 10, 8 or even 6
Tying thread: Black
Tail: Cock pheasant dyed yellow
Rib: Very fine gold wire
Body: Bright yellow floss
Body hackle: Golden ginger/olive cock, palmered
Wings: Grizzle hackle points dyed yellow
Front hackle: Olive badger cock
Head: Black

I have no reason to doubt that it would work just as well elsewhere. Sadly my own flytying skills do not extend to fully winged flies such as this.

It was whilst Tim and Patrick were fishing the Trou de Bombe during this visit that I was forced into relaxing my 'no nymphs' rule as they were determined to catch a couple of fish that defeated all other methods. The attempts to catch these tricky characters also lead to great hilarity with one or other fishing for a trout he could not see whilst the other 'bomb aimed' for him – 'left a bit, a bit further out – no you've lined him' and so on. They failed.

Riparian Owners' Association

Laurent, the tenant of the fishing at St Pol after the death of Tante Odette, is a man of action. Encountering a continual deterioration of the fishing there, he commissioned an in-depth report from an English specialist which suggested a number of potential issues and provided some possible solutions.

Feeling that the results of this survey might be of interest to other riparian owners he gradually drew together sufficient of these to form an association. We joined as soon as we heard of it – which was sadly a bit late as many things were already in the pipeline before we even knew of its existence.

The way we got to hear of the association was through meeting Laurent, which in itself was via a very convoluted route. The aforementioned Patrick and his wife, Zanna, had met him fishing in Scotland and somehow the conversation had got on to chalkstreams and from there to French chalkstreams whereupon he said he knew someone with fishing on the Andelle and on it went from there. Laurent promptly contacted us and we signed up.

Apart from the extraordinary achievement of getting such a diverse band to join together for the mutual good, Laurent had also persuaded them to subscribe to the production of a book on the Andelle and its history, to be professionally produced. We duly subscribed. Sadly the book, *Abécédaire Amoureux de l'Andelle*, was too far down the line and the few contributions we made were too late for inclusion and our village is virtually non-existent on the map of the river – almost suggesting that there is no fishing along this stretch. This may turn out to have unforeseen advantages! Our name was hand-written amongst the subscribers – we were that late! Nonetheless it is a fine production.

We went along to the first meeting we could after joining the association which was held in a local village hall. At last we got to meet some of our neighbours, amongst whom, we were amazed to find, were an English couple. Amazed because it is rare to even see a car with UK plates here and we certainly did not know of any 'Brits' living nearby. It was surprising that we had not heard about them.

This couple had bought a delightful fortified farmhouse on the Andelle that I had briefly considered when browsing French property magazines. I had rejected it as the fishing was on a very narrow stretch upstream of where we now live and which I could not see supporting a really good head of fish. They had done amazing work on the river, but above all on the house, converting it to a superior Chambre d'Hôte. Sadly they have now sold and moved on.

One initiative the association undertook was an attempt to raise indigenous Andelle trout in a hatchery and spread this fine strain more widely through the river. The English couple volunteered to build the hatching pens on their land and we were 'volunteered' to provide the breeding fish as our beat was thought to hold the best stock of true Andelle trout because the beat had not been stocked. We were not in residence when the fish were captured but were assured that they had found some fine specimens to start the experiment. Sadly this initiative was very short-lived as the very first winter the breeding stock escaped to be seen no more. I wonder if they found their way home?

This was unfortunately just one of several blows which made this into a very short-lived Association. Chief of these was Laurent giving up his lease at St Pol, as he had been very much the driving force behind the whole enterprise.

Others also moved away from the area. Too many were weekenders from Paris and no-one had the energy to take up where Laurent left off – they could not see the benefit of mutual support when it came to the imposition of rules from government, with regard to poachers, control of vermin, and indeed general advice and research into reduction in flylife and such like.

It is so often the case when people are giving their time freely that such efforts come to naught but this seemed to have so much going for it. We even had members who were vets and scientists to add professional weight to our arguments. To emphasise our loss, we have now been imposed a set of rules by the powers that be (well-meaning on this occasion) regarding bank protection and now have no voice to speak on our behalf. Laurent meantime is President of the world-famous Fario Club, started originally by Charles Ritz.

Building Works

Reading the title of this chapter you will be expecting to hear of a trail of disasters and delays – but you are to be disappointed.

We have gradually taken the house in hand over the twenty-odd years we have been here but time had taught us to think hard before changing some of the original installation. For example the ugly fireplace which had been top of our list to change proved to light so easily (one fire-lighter and just logs – not even any kindling) and to draw so efficiently that it escaped the chop. The unattractive brown and white tiled floor in the hall and the black and white marble chip in the drawing room also survived as they helped keep the house so cool in the summer. We softened the worst of their appearance by laying simple, natural rugs (the left-overs from an exhibition stand) over them. The same approach has been taken upstairs with rugs laid over the very ordinary wooden floors.

In the last three years we have undertaken some fairly major improvements. Most of the tradesmen we have used have remained the same throughout and the standard of work has been impeccable, with sympathetic handling of an old building thrown in! This has made a great difference to the outcome. I do not think that they ever understood why we wanted to keep a slightly dilapidated look but they did their best to suppress their Norman desire for immaculate tidiness sufficiently to deliver a look we were able to bear.

Monsieur Serval the electrician proved to be a life-saver but first signs were not encouraging. We had problems with the pump that supplied all our water from our own bore-hole. Incidentally whisky here tastes better than anywhere I know, when taken with a little of this pure, cold water. We have never dared to have the water tested, as we should by law, as we are sure it would fail, and yet it is wonderful and to date no-one has been ill. Monsieur Serval arrived, promptly (something we found common to all the workmen we employed – it must be another Norman trait), a dark, heavy-browed man with a drooping, luxuriant moustache and face to match, he was pessimism personified. Years later we learnt that he had a gentle, dry sense of humour but this was not currently in evidence.

The usual sucking in of teeth left the impression that he was not going to be able to fix the pump then and there, and he showed no great desire to do so. And yet, when it came down to it, he not only mended it, via a very clever 'bodge', but explained where the problem lay, how it could be improved upon and avoided in the future. We have learnt that as a race the Normans are *méfiant* [mistrustful] until they get to know you but that you can eventually build up their trust to the point where they become incredibly faithful and where nothing is too much trouble. Monsieur Serval rescued us on more than one occasion with the dreaded pump breaking down, always at a weekend with guests on their way and on one occasion, at Easter. We were of course entirely dependent on this pump, as without it we had no water at all – the house has no water storage, everything is pumped up from way beneath (we do not actually know exactly where the source is). The hand-pump in the garden had not worked in living memory and indeed now hosted the nest of a family of blue tits. Monsieur Serval however never let us down.

The latest chapter in the saga of the pump resulted in the cellar being under a foot of water and the pump still furiously doing its job and adding to the depth whilst being totally immersed. It turned out that the small header tank, which dated from the original works in the 1950s, had rusted through to the extent that the whole of the bottom fell through and the pump knew no better than to continue. Luckily the floor of the cellar is of beaten earth and the flood dispersed within a day. Everything had to be replaced as the electric pump was not designed to work under water!

The other tradesmen were built in a similar mould, though perhaps a little more cheerful. We had a wonderful mason, Monsieur Lemercier, who was a sort of project manager for us but whose own skills lay in the sympathetic restoration of the timber framed buildings. A slow and soft-spoken man, he always appeared to think more than he spoke but when he did it was worth listening. He would go out of his way to find the right, old beam to replace a rotten one and, when restoring what is now my studio, he was almost in tears when he could not source an old beam of over four metres in length. Needless to say he eventually did. He was unable to bear the thought of installing a new beam.

When we first bought the house I noticed that the beam forming the lintel over the cellar door had a hole right through it. I asked Monsieur Lemercier to replace it. Upon inspection he told me there was no need and that the remaining wood was so strong that it would hold for a very long time. In my ignorance I insisted – it was a big hole – and replace it he did.

When the job was complete he asked me to come and have a look. He showed me three chain saw blades lying beside the door and explained that the oak of the beam was so hard they had broken all three in cutting through it. I had learnt my lesson – oak becomes, with age, as hard as iron.

The studio has been created from a small bothy in the garden which seems to have been multi-purpose originally. There is a very fine brick bread oven which dominates the interior and there had been a large sink (now removed) which was presumably for household washing as there is the hand pump outside. Built into the outside walls there are small 'rooms' apparently for rabbits and possibly a pig. It was common practice for families to raise a pig each year and the slaughter and butchery of this animal was a major event with the whole family involved making sausages, black pudding and curing the hams – no part of the pig was wasted.

The back portion of the building consisted of another small room which had hatches at ground level for the passage of chickens leading to an outside run and for pigeons at a higher level.

Also for this studio he suggested some antique tomettes (small terracotta tiles) for the floor that he happened to have in his garage, and of which there were just enough. He then set his apprentice to clean up these tiles, a job which required endless patience. The end result is so much nicer than the modern equivalent would have been.

His rendering and the colouring thereof was a work of art and the first job he did (re-building the back wall of the house when we first bought it) has not moved at all in over twenty years. He is that great rarity, a builder who when he takes an initiative it always turns out to have been a good idea. His note-taking consisted of the odd scribble on a scrap of paper and the internet was a mystery to him. But what a craftsman! He also turned out to be Monsieur Lapointe's nephew – Lapointe, The Pony Man, was related to or knew everyone – a precious contact.

The final major player in the team was Luke. We ended up with him by mistake and with considerable trepidation. We had had several plumbers round to give us a quotation when one evening Luke knocked on our door. We knew him well – he was our next door neighbour and he was in his twenties. We knew that his father had been an electrician as he had lived in the house behind us where Luke now lived with his young family. The father had, according to local gossip, won the Lotto, and he had won '*le grand lot*' – in any case he had moved away and given the house to Luke. He had come, he said, because he had seen plumbers' vans outside and wondered if he might quote for the job we were clearly preparing. We did not even know he was a plumber so were a trifle embarrassed but felt we had to give him a shot. But if he quoted and was competitive we were between a rock and a hard place because he was so close we virtually had to accept his quote – and what if he was no good? This of course is what did transpire except that he *was* good – very good. Furthermore he could do virtually anything – it turned out that he was a trained electrician and was building himself a new house, doing all the trades. He ended up doing many different things for us – he was even prepared to tackle a blocked septic tank, nobody's favourite job.

Wonderful though the roofer was also, we hardly got to know him as he came, did the job quickly and left – and it was always perfect. The boss would even visit a week or two after completion to ensure his and our complete satisfaction with the job his men had done. The French are tremendously skilled with slate roofing of which there are some wonderful examples around here – the church spire at La Feuillie which is a very tall, thin needle shape is one such and the slate-work is spectacular.

Much the same could be said of the carpenter, a slightly effete man whose standards were such that we were forced to bring him down to earth when he proposed a bench of virtually Chippendale standards of design and finish when we simply wanted somewhere to sit to take off our boots in the fishing room. I think he is a cabinet maker manqué. Once agreed he simply arrived with his work pre-prepared, fitted it and left.

All this is very different to the popular view of the French builder. It is true that the works overall took rather longer than desirable (actually a lot longer) but that was because we were not there to drive them on.

Gardening

Once we had agreed to disagree with Stallone over the way we wanted our garden to look, we decided that the simplest solution was to find a local garden contractor who wouldn't have the time for 'good ideas'.

On one of our Saturday trips to the market in Ry we had noticed a man selling not just the usual bedding plants one always finds on the market, but also a few shrubs. We subsequently noticed that his van stated that he was indeed a garden contractor. So we approached this ruddy-cheeked man (good sign – he spent his day outside) and asked if he might be interested in looking after our simple garden. He agreed to come and have a look and, after a very brief description of what we wanted – mowing the grass once a week in the main growing season, strimming the rougher areas and cutting hedges twice a year – he wrote us a quote and we agreed on the spot with payment on invoice once a year in arrears. Quite an expression of trust.

This has been a relationship that has been entirely without problems to this day. Not only has Monsieur Compin (for that is his name) done everything we agreed but he has, without being asked, weed-killed the gravel drive, pruned the roses that weren't there when he started and caught the moles which appear regularly (driven up into the garden we suspect by rises in the river levels).

Furthermore he undertook to improve the apple trees which had become far too large and has had his mowing greatly impeded by the increasing numbers of shrubs and trees we have planted not to mention the huge number of fallen apples as there are far too many for our needs.

Despite our initial determination not to increase the amount of work in the garden, many people have given us plants and trees over the years. These have included some unusual trees such as the 'Golden Rain Tree' (*Koelreuteria paniculata*), given to me for my fiftieth birthday. This tree carries beautiful yellow panicles of flowers followed by seed pods rather like Chinese lanterns, though it did take ten years to flower for the first time. This we planted to hide the house directly behind ours, a job it is now doing admirably.

Cercidiphyllum Japonica adds a touch of the Orient to the glorious local autumn colour. This exotic tree, which was also a gift, gives pleasure all the year round as its leaves are an unusual heart shape and drift delicately in the slightest breeze and so sneaked through the 'no more planting' rule.

On a more sensible note we planted a mirabelle plum. These trees produce small yellow plums with purple splodges which make the most delicious jam imaginable and we had always been determined to have one.

To date we have not managed more than a couple of pots per annum. Either the crop has been too small (or even non-existent) or the birds have got there first. To our shame we have had to buy our mirabelles on the market where they are generally to be found as most people who have a mirabelle tree end up with too much fruit. Where did we go wrong?

Here I should add a note of caution to anyone wanting to buy one of these trees in England. Friends did indeed buy a 'mirabelle' in the UK and ended up with yellow plums alright, but plums the size of a Victoria – altogether something else. *Caveat emptor.*

Soon after moving in we discovered that there were a number of gardens locally open to the public and, on visiting one or two, it became evident that this was an area where roses thrived. I have always loved old-fashioned French shrub roses and couldn't resist planting one or two, despite their single flowering, as the scent is unparalleled as is the beauty of the flowers. As I write the glorious perfume of the deliciously named *Cuisse de Nymphe Emue* (much less fun in English as Maiden's Blush) is wafting through the window of my studio.

Monsieur Compin has taken all this in his stride and has now added the task of cleaning, re-filling and re-planting the window boxes and tubs in front of the house. Right from day one I had an obsession that we should do as so many of the locals do and have the simplest, single, bright red geraniums in the window boxes: and so we have done. They seem to me to look just right.

We have never had a cross word (actually Compin hardly says a word at all) – though I was tempted to say something when he treated our choisya as a topiary ball. He just turns up, puts on his ear defenders and gets on with it. Sadly he has just announced his forthcoming retirement but in the same breath assures us he has found his replacement, so typical of the man.

The climate at Cercy, as mentioned, is very similar to that of the south of England, often at one day's remove. It does have slightly colder winters and can be liable to a very late frost – one year so late that even the apples did not survive it and we had not one. On one occasion we even had snow falling on Easter day.

Summers are very slightly warmer overall and the area is prone to electrical storms, as discussed elsewhere. However there is generally sufficient rain-fall to support an old local saying that 'we never water in Normandy'. Naturally being so close to the river the water table is high and the ground very fertile – gardening is easy, just plant and watch it (whatever it is) grow. The chalk ensures that the winter rain is released slowly throughout the year and even now as I write the longest drought for many years has not yet reduced the grass to straw.

River Maintenance

Clearly the river was not going to look after itself, particularly once we had established just how little Stallone actually considered his job entailed.

The fencing of the banks had brought undoubted benefits. Without the cattle grazing, the wild flowers were not the only things to benefit and grow with renewed vigour. We were going to have to strim at least every two weeks in the growing season to deal with the luxuriant growth of weeds, nettles, thistles etc. This would have the added benefit of eventually killing the nettles as these invasive plants do eventually surrender if continually cut (they still haven't!). Stallone agreed to do this 'extra' at an hourly rate, which slightly terrified us as, with his neat perfectionism it could take a week to do the job to his satisfaction.

This did indeed prove to be the case. We needed to find someone who knew exactly how we wanted it done without being told each time and who would be perhaps a little less precise than Stallone. We needed to ask Monsieur Lapointe – he would know someone. He did!

'You need Robert,' he said 'he can't work with other people in a team and he is usually available'. We asked where we could find this Robert and were pointed, inevitably, to Arlette's. Marthe headed up to the café and asked Arlette if she knew a Robert. Practically before she had finished asking a huge man in a sleeveless vest and clutching a glass of red wine (it was ten in the morning) came over and said, 'I'm Robert'. Marthe told him what was needed and before she had finished he had put down his glass and was heading for the door with her, despite her protestations that he should finish his glass.

To start with we were slightly wary of this bear of a man with his reputation that he couldn't work with others. However he turned out to be perfect as he would do exactly what he was told and do it quickly, and well. His strength, which was considerable, made him the ideal man for the job (and others that gradually came his way). He only had to be shown once how we wanted the strimming done, leaving a good fringe at river-side, and he had it done in no time. He quickly understood that we just wanted a simple path and no more, leaving the river bank as wild as possible. All our attempts to convince him to wear the right protective clothing proved fruitless – the sleeveless vest prevailed in all weathers, though he was prepared to wear goggles, probably to keep us quiet. He enjoyed a good chat (and a beer) when he had finished but seemed to have a clear idea of when to leave (unlike Stallone).

He lived with just his cousin in a huge house that had been a restaurant when we first moved into the village. We never discovered if this was some form of social housing but it seemed unlikely that he had actually bought this huge place. Contacting him always proved a problem as his door-bell did not work and he had no letter-box. Furthermore Arlette had banned him (for fighting we presumed) from the café so when we wanted him we usually asked Monsieur Lapointe who always seemed to be able to find him – usually within minutes. Alternatively a message left with his cousin, when she could be found, would bring him running like a naughty school boy saying he had been told 'La Dame' (Marthe) needed to see him.

Stallone, who never usually had a good word to say about any job he had not done himself, grudgingly admitted that Robert had 'done quite a good job' on the river bank. One of his delights seemed to be reporting to us that we had a tree either dead, or leaning dangerously over the river, or both. Usually he would arrange to do this 'extra' himself. However when we decided that too much of the river had become unfishable with over-hanging branches (actually Marthe had – I rather enjoyed the challenge), we decided that a contractor needed to be called in.

We had always bought the considerable quantity of firewood we used from the Frères Routier who were conveniently based in the village and had their woodyard on the edge of town. These brothers, in their sixties, lived alone and, as far as we could tell, unmarried – one brother was rumoured to have a girlfriend. They looked almost as alike as to be twins and what few gruff words they did say were, to me anyway, pretty near incomprehensible. They had the other disadvantage of being as difficult to get hold of as Robert. However they did have an answer-phone and they were clearly the men for the job. A deal was done which would end up with us having a load of extra firewood and a fat bill but a fishable river.

By August most years the luxuriant weed-growth would be showing its head above the level of the water and began to interfere with the fishing. The weed-cutting dates, discussed elsewhere, were unsuitable and this needed addressing. Had the Riparian Owners' Association survived, here was something we could have fought for together – coordinated and agreed dates.

By now the commune bridge over the river was in a sorry state with the timber mostly rotten and the local lads having great fun throwing as much of it as they could into the river. We discovered the problem – the bridge fell exactly on the dividing line between two different départements and, of course, each one thought it was the other's responsibility. Eventually the repairs were undertaken (we never knew who gave in first). This was a relief as it was the only way to access our fishing from the right (preferred) bank and it looked like we might have to cross on the bare girders which were the only sound part left. Sadly, whilst the woodwork of the replacement was of the highest quality, no-one thought to treat the timbers with any form of preservative so as I write the whole exercise has just had to be carried out again.

Nature Watch

Ownership of this stretch of delightful chalkstream has provided a fascinating opportunity to observe the wildlife locally, and it has produced some surprises too.

Birdlife both by the river and in the garden is wonderfully diverse including many species which have become relatively scarce in the UK. We have recently started to feed the garden birds to see if we can get a better look at some of them. I realise we are doing it all wrong by feeding in the spring and summer when we are here and they don't need it, and not feeding in the winter when we are away and they do need it. But we love to see the great variety of birds that visit the feeders which are sited outside the kitchen window and by my studio, within sight of my desk.

Fortunately there are kingfishers on the river – I know feelings are mixed as they do take fish, but who can resist seeing them? They seem to be very territorial as we only ever catch a glimpse of them along one stretch at the bottom of our beat. There has been one year when they disappeared and not one was seen but fortunately they have reappeared. I believe they are susceptible to a hard winter.

It was rare to fish without hearing the mewing cries of a pair of buzzards, circling above the river. I know these birds are not popular with farmers but I love to see them and fortunately there seem to be plenty around.

Less fortunately there are, inevitably, herons and cormorants. The herons are not too numerous and, I believe, do little damage in our case. Besides they are, to me, a fundamental part of the chalkstream scene and I would miss them if they weren't there.

The cormorants come in greater numbers, though perhaps less frequently. They are, as in England, a protected species. This is another example of someone sitting in an office in town and having no comprehension of the effects of his edict when applied. We are able to apply for Stallone to shoot them on our land but the regulations limit his total kill across all the properties he manages to seven cormorants. What good is that going to do? I cannot believe that this bird is in any way endangered as they seem to be numerous wherever one goes. Unlike the heron I believe they are really damaging to a fishery – they arrive, often mob-handed, and take fish of a reasonable size and in quantity, then leave before we can do anything. I have only ever seen the herons take very small fish and they are solitary birds here.

For many years a barn owl used to roost on our outside floodlight and only left, under protest, when we drove up at night and our headlights disturbed him. Sadly we no longer see him and the pile of distinctive droppings below the light no longer appear, though I still hear him call at nightfall.

Naturally swallows and martins are common in season, swooping over the river like squadrons of Spitfires as they 'hawk' the mayflies, sometimes expertly picking them off the the river whilst barely breaking the surface tension of the water. I have, on occasion, even seen them take a mayfly head-on and actually heard the click of their beaks as they took the insect's head off, the wings fluttering down, neatly clipped from the body. The flying skills of these birds are to be seen to be believed. I often take the field glasses which hang by the front door to scan the river for swallows and take their presence as an indication that a hatch is on. Fishermen are then dispatched forthwith to the river.

Sadly they are not infallible. I am not alone I am sure in having hooked a swallow on the dry fly. In my case the Mayfly I was fishing was taken in the air and unfortunately taken down deep to the extent that I was obliged to put the bird out of its misery. I have also heard of similar cases where the artificial fly had been picked off the surface of the water. Maybe our imitations are better than we realise.

Swans can be the bane of the fisherman's life on the chalkstreams, tearing up the weed in huge quantities, always in residence on the pool you want to fish and attacking you (particularly if you have a dog) when nesting. Fortunately we do not have swans on the Andelle and it was with shock and horror that I suddenly saw one appear from nowhere. To my great relief he seemed to be on his own and only stayed a couple of days. He then disappeared and was never seen again. Long may this situation last.

Every year without fail a pair of mallard manage to raise a clutch of ducklings and their survival rate seems pretty good – until that is, the opening day of La Chasse. This is a day to stay indoors. Everyone who owns a gun seems to be out and blazing off at everything on the wing or on the ground, whatever its size (and legality as game). Monsieur Dumont, as the tenant farmer, has the shooting rights over the fields either side of the river and most of the local equivalent of the Council join him in this mass slaughter (he is a councillor). I fear that not too many of the duck survive for long although clearly at least one pair do so each year. The shoot have even constructed hides along the river to aid the extinction of these trusting birds who will continue to circle back to their 'home', guns or no.

As to game (real game that is) it is surprising that there are very few game-birds to be seen. In all the time we have been here I have seen precisely one pheasant and two partridges, though I do hear the distinctive pheasant call regularly. The terrain should be ideal for partridge but maybe the answer lies in the paragraph above.

As I have mentioned before, wild boar do come down to the river to drink. But we have never seen these shy creatures despite often being by the river in the gloaming when they tend to come out, though we have seen them on the road. More surprisingly I have never seen a fox and only once have I seen a rabbit – extraordinary to anyone who lives in England. This is clearly a sign that the French applied myxomatosis to the ultimate conclusion.

One extraordinary incident occurred in our second year at Cercy. I was sitting on one of the benches by the river, smoking my pipe and idly watching the river for signs of a fish coming on the rise when I spotted a black rabbit floating past. Clearly dead and obviously a domesticated one, my interest was piqued. What could have caused this? It seemed unlikely that its cage run would be open to the water's edge and that it had fallen in and drowned. Shortly afterwards a second, this time brown, rabbit floated past – the plot thickened. Over the next few minutes a further three passed me, all dead. No solution came to my mind at the time nor has anything ever to come to light. This strange event will forever remain a mystery though I suspect foul play!

Happily there are no grey squirrels in France, though there are apparently concerns that they may be on their way across the border from Italy. We do however very occasionally see a red one which is always a pleasure.

In common with the UK we seem to see fewer butterflies by the year. We had one bonanza year when we saw both quantity but also variety but I fear that was a one-off and it is usually cabbage whites and the occasional red admiral that we see in Cercy. I presume they suffer from whatever ails the river flies.

On one of his visits to fish here, Tim Bridge reported one evening that he had seen an otter eating a trout on the far bank by the Trou de Bombe. None of us had ever seen one so we asked Stallone who expressed great surprise and some scepticism. He returned the following day and assured us that the Bailiff had told him that there were no otters in the region – 'not for fifty kilometres around'. Tim is a very experienced fisherman and countryman and I did not doubt that if he said he had seen an otter, he had seen an otter. Some years later the same thing happened and so, even though I haven't seen one myself, I state with confidence that there are otters on the Andelle.

Putting the River to Bed

Autumn is here. Even though we are in late September the trees on the escarpment across the valley are resolutely hanging on to their leaves and there is, as yet, very little autumn colouring – green predominates still. Usually by this time of year the deciduous trees of the forest are ablaze with ochres, oranges, yellows and browns but the long, dry summer seems to have confused nature's clock. Surrounded as we are by the superbly maintained Forêts Dominiales – the state-owned forests – this time of year can be truly spectacular as oak, beech and chestnuts predominate.

Walking the river for the last time this season, I note what needs to be done through the winter and before the fishing re-opens in mid-March. I can see that once again the cattle have leant on our fences at a number of points and the barbed wire will need to be re-stretched using the special 'key' that Stallone had himself made – and which he and Monsieur Coligny fight over all year round, the farmer insisting he will do the job and demanding the key, and Stallone demanding its return when it is clear the job is not going to be done.

The banks along the Home Straight have been excessively poached by the cattle during the previous winter when they have got through the flimsy electric fence. Four drainage ditches enter the river along this stretch and so the banks have never dried out sufficiently to harden and build up naturally. We will have to tackle this soon, but how? I think we will have to import some hard-core and top-soil, fill the water rat burrows and compact the poached areas. We will also have to provide some simple plank bridges over the drainage ditches. This is a big job – not for this winter.

We have previously done some fairly extensive bank re-building. Sylvestre drove stakes into the river bed along a stretch of some fifty yards at the top end of our beat, just below the bridge. He wove lengths of willow in and out of these stakes and protected them with chicken wire. Back-filled with earth, this section of bank was then planted with saplings so that the roots would help strengthen the 'new' profile. He further added some wild flowers, particularly flag irises and stood back to admire his handy-work.

Sadly some five years later all that remains is the row of stakes behind which the river is already eating into the bank. They stand clear of the bank like crooked teeth with the river flowing behind them. The trees he planted have flourished to the extent that several have had to be felled in order to give fishermen some elbow room but the yellow irises give pleasure each spring. Overall, though, this experiment has been a failure. Do we try to repair or redo this work? I do sometimes wonder whether it is not best to let the river decide which way it will flow. So often work done to direct the flow and to deposit silt in a different area fails in the long term.

Reaching Marthe's Corner I can see that the bench is in danger of falling into the river this coming winter as the current has gradually eaten away the bank as it was deflected off the left bank to hit the inside of the bend leading into Dark Run. The name of this stretch was, I realised now, something of a misnomer as the felling of many of the trees on the opposite bank has let in much more light. I notice that these clearances have also revealed a number of alders that are dead or dying and which will need to be felled this winter too – I must mark them with Stallone.

This will mean another job for the Routier brothers and more firewood for our store – no bad thing given how much we get through. We seem to have a fire most nights, even in August, as the temperature drops very quickly once the sun goes behind the hill opposite. This effect is most noticeable in good weather when it is not too humid.

Hopefully the extra sunlight getting through once these trees are felled might encourage some fish to take up residence in this hitherto barren stretch. Dark Run has hardly produced a fish in the whole time we have owned the property and only 'sardines' are ever seen to rise in it.

The weeds have been a menace this year with the water so low early in the spring and followed by a hot, dry summer, they have had their heads in the air for much of the fishing season. The regulations regarding the cutting of weed on the Andelle are similar to the south of England with clearance only allowed on specific dates. However there were only two allowed sets of dates and each over a very short period. We have long since come to the conclusion that it is pointless carrying out this back-breaking job. The first date is too early, before the weeds have grown to any great extent, and the second is too late, when the fishing season was virtually over. Hence we leave nature to do the job and scour out the dead weed in the winter, a job which she does most efficiently year after year.

Not for the first time I vow to replace the old white benches with the wider, natural oak benches that Stallone has built for us. I also feel the need to add a new one at Amen Corner which, being on a sharp bend, will give a great viewing spot to linger whilst awaiting a hatch, with lengthy views up and downstream.

Studying the gravelly runs where the trout dig their redds, I am satisfied that they run clean and bright and need no attention. Stallone has tried for many years to persuade us to employ a local man to harrow the gravel with a heavy horse, but we had never really felt the need. The number of small fish we see every year suggests that nature is producing quite enough youngsters for the very light pressure of fishing we provide. I have also heard mixed reports on the efficacy of this method, and indeed the side-effects. The only really effective way of breaking up calcified lumps of gravel is by back-breakingly doing it by hand with a garden fork or spade.

We looked for a suitable spot to plant the weeping willow we had given ourselves as a wedding anniversary present. Just above the 'Trou de Bombe' looked like the answer. It would not interfere with the fishing as the fast, shallow run here has never been known to hold a fish and it will, in time, provide a wonderful shady spot in which to lie and watch for a rise above or below – even if it might be our grandchildren who enjoy the benefits.

Reaching the bottom of the beat I spot the now almost invisible hut in the thicket behind the bottom bench. It is covered with briars and is now almost inaccessible as Stallone, for reasons known only to him, had decided to finish the fence just short of the hut. Nonetheless I feel it might have its uses. If one was caught out at the far end of the beat when one of the summer thunder-storms suddenly broke, then one could at least stay reasonably dry – most people do not set out on a summer's day with a waterproof when the fishing is so close to home.

Years earlier I had tried to repair it with a visiting friend but our efforts had not lasted and something more fundamental was needed. I think we should combine a proper repair with the installation of a Norfolk gate at that point (where it has always been needed) and the extension of the fence so that it passes round the back of the hut before going down to the river's edge. Next year?

I might try some of those fly-boards – I have heard of people having good results with them.

To quote Haig-Brown: 'A river never sleeps'.

THE END

Postscript

I have described our property as 'paradise' and have hinted through this little book at the reasons for this love affair. In summary it represents, in so many ways, the best of both French and English cultures.

We have deliberately kept the house simple and somewhat rustic – it is in no way 'precious,' meaning it is easy to open and close both for each visit but also for the start and end of the season when we close the house down completely.

As we do not, and never will, let the house or the fishing, there is no pressure for manicured banks along the river nor for hotel-standard accommodation. It remains very much a home – our home. For the same reason there is no need to stock with young fish and our guests still fish for wild, pure-bred, Andelle chalkstream trout, some of which attain considerable size – all in all, a rare delight these days.

This is a haven of calm. There is virtually no traffic noise, particularly noticeable in the house, no light pollution, with starry skies at night and few signs or sounds of humans (apart, of course, from daily interruptions from Stallone). The locals, once we penetrated their natural restraint, have proved to be loyal, kind, hard-working and, above all, friendly. The locality retains a charming somewhat old-fashioned atmosphere and is largely unspoilt. Apart from Rouen itself, there is not too much aggressive development, and nearby are some of the prettiest villages in France. The villages around us all still have weekly street markets and, as yet, the march of the supermarket is contained, though the threat is there.

It is close enough to London and the south of England to make weekends eminently do-able which is important in appealing to our daughters, their husbands and their friends. Increasingly they are now filling the house with their own parties, just as we have done for so long.

Many of our friends have been returning year after year and the whole place is full of memories, of long friendships, of hilarity, of opera round a blazing fire, of the usual exaggerated fish sizes and associated banter. The fishing record book is a hard copy of all this and serves to settle arguments of dates, of fellow guests and of course of the aforementioned fish sizes, along with photographic evidence of much of the above.

All this would be very hard, if not impossible, to find anywhere else and I believe I am entitled to call it paradise.